PARENT AND TEEN
TEAMED FOR SUCCESS

PARENT AND TEEN
TEAMED FOR SUCCESS

RONALD JOHN ZIRKER

Deseret Book Company
Salt Lake City, Utah

First printing in paperbound edition, August 1990

Library of Congress Cataloging-in-Publication Data

Zirker, Ronald J.
    Parent and teen.

    Includes index
        1. Parenting. 2. Parent and child. 3. Adolescence.
I. Title.
HQ755.8.Z57 1985   306.8'74   84-29785
ISBN 0-87579-363-0

Printed in the United States of America

10   9   8   7   6   5   4   3   2   1

Contents

Acknowledgments

I would like to thank my wife and partner in parenting, without whom this manuscript might still be only a collection of notes and lectures. I appreciate the hours of typing, editing, and organizing—but most of all, I appreciate the twenty-five years of adventure we have shared in our life together. Without Sherri's encouragement, support, and belief in my stewardship, this manuscript might never have been written.

I appreciate my children: Katherine Anne Hawkins, Carolyn Ruth, Connie Sue, David John, and Steven Robert. My thanks to each of them for allowing me to invade the privacy of their lives and to share certain details of our lives together.

I thank my parents, John Eugene and Pearl Wall, who provided the pattern of love and devotion that shaped my life and set the example, and my older brother, Kenneth Eugene, and sister, Bonnie DeGraff, whom I have loved and looked up to all my life.

I thank my wife's family and particularly her parents, Robert C. and Lora Magnusson, and Joseph E. Potts and Ronald and Bette Doxey, who shared insights and contributed support.

Thanks are due also to several editors and typists, including Lavina Fielding Anderson, Susan Mendelsohn, Katherine Hawkins, and particularly my wife, Sherri, who organized my lectures, notes, and ponderings into a readable manuscript.

1

Parents' Responsibilities

Years ago, when the youngest of our five children was about two years old, I learned one of the most important lessons of my life—one that would set the tone for all my future relationships with my children.

Steven was full of energy, full of ideas, full of curiosity, and full of charm. A flash of his winsome grin and arms wrapped tightly around my leg would usually melt my heart completely. One day, however, I was exasperated beyond limit. A spank aimed at his bottom landed right where I meant it to. Startled, then righteously indignant, Steven faced me squarely, hands on his hips, his head tilted up to mine, and he roared: "I'm going to tell Father on you!"

I knelt to his level and said, "But Steven, I *am* your father."

He glared unyieldingly. "No sir. You're my dad. I'm going to tell Father on you."

And with that, he turned on his heel and left. It took a moment for his words to sink in. Then I hurried after him—anxious to continue the conversation. He didn't even remember what he had said. But I did. In fact, I couldn't forget it.

I had long been acquainted with scriptures that counsel parents in their important responsibility (Ephesians 6; D&C 68:25; 93:36-40) and record the problems that result when that responsibility has been neglected (Exodus 34: 6-7; 1 Samuel 1-3). I held a temple recommend and went to the temple as often as I could, served on a high council, performed my duties as a school psychologist with integrity, belonged to several service organizations in the community, and had a wonderful relationship with Sherri, my wife. Our home was almost paid for, we had a two-years' supply of food, and we held family prayer and family home evening regularly. I felt satisfied and contented with myself and my life.

Steven's announcement had jarred my contentment and triggered a private search that marked a turning point in my life. Just what *was* my stewardship as a parent? What was I expected to accomplish with it?

My search created in me a new awareness of parent-child dynamics. As a high councilor, I was assigned to work with the Young Adults and the Indian Placement program. Over the years I saw Young Adults with energy and purpose take positions of leadership, marry fine companions, and start families with children born under the covenant. I also observed Young Adults who wandered aimlessly from job to job, married quickly, and ended up struggling, sometimes unsuccessfully, with unhappy, immature marriages.

Our family has taken in many foster children for varying lengths of time. One Indian Placement student, Lori, came to us from an adoring father who wrote often, encouraging her to "learn all you can where such wonderful opportunities are given you to grow." She became a part of our family, filling our home with goodwill and laughter. She learned to sing and to play the violin and piano. She became a cheerleader and a fine student. Other foster children, however, stole our property, mocked our family's values, resisted all efforts at friendship—and some even ended up in Juvenile Hall. Many of these children received little or no communication from their parents. We concluded that Lori's father had magnified his stewardship by sending her to us for greater purposes, whereas others had hoped to use the placement program to absolve their responsibility for their children.

I remember one teenage girl I'll call Becky who was referred to me for counseling. She had just been released from the hospital where she had been taken after an attempted suicide. She was so hostile that I could do nothing for her during the first few visits. She maintained a front of silence and belligerence. Finally, tossing aside the usual questions and therapy techniques, I felt impressed to ask, "Has anyone ever told you they loved you?"

My question broke the silence. Huge, racking sobs filled the room as she shook her head over and over again. In a faltering voice she said, "And I've never told anybody I loved them."

Her story gradually came out. Her parents had been killed in an accident when she was about three years old, and she had lived in foster homes and with relatives from that time on. She felt like a burden, totally alone.

Our visits became regular and productive. I helped convince her that she could make something of her life, helped her gain control over her study habits, and challenged her to make friends and get involved in school activities.

Then I moved fifteen hundred miles away. A letter was forwarded to me. It read:

> Dear Mr. Zirker:
>   You are just like all the rest. I was only a job to you, wasn't I? You didn't care any more than the others did.
>   Becky

The letter broke my heart. I didn't have the stewardship to offer her the continuity she so desperately needed; the courts decided such jurisdiction and were impersonal in their assessment of her needs. There was no affidavit for her tears—or mine.

I wept again when I saw a foster son deported for theft and another placed in the county detention hall for trying to leave town with a stolen automobile and the neighbor's daughter. These young men, both age fourteen, had tried to fit into our neighborhood. They felt angry and frustrated when friends' parents shut their doors against them. They had acquired only limited academic skills, and their failures in school further humiliated them. Suffering from low self-esteem, they grew so deviant in their behavior that they lost the freedom to mingle with those who might have helped.

I observed that parents of teenagers felt great frustrations. Their ability to control their children had diminished the minute those sons or daughters discovered they could do anything an adult could—drive a car, get a job, come and go at will, even wear adult-size clothing. Trouble accelerated. Parents who expected good grades, adherence to a curfew, and some measure of a moral code—in fact, who made any attempts to structure their teenagers—were met with defiance.

As a counselor, I was often asked by parents, "Where did I go wrong? He never used to be this way." This question was asked by nice guys, like myself. Others asked me why I hadn't done *my* job better, why teachers hadn't done their part better. Society was to blame, everyone else was at fault, even their teen: "He never would listen, never has given me any peace since the day he was born!"

When my wife was called to work with the Young Women in the ward, she came home from a meeting with Elaine Cannon, the new general president of the organization. Sister Cannon knew that Latter-day Saint teens were having problems: drugs, running away, suicides, abortions—and that the girls were getting into trouble much younger, even at Primary age. She felt two things would help young women avoid such pitfalls: a concerned priesthood holder and a woman the girl could love and respect enough to emulate. Could girls find that example in their homes? In their mothers and fathers?

As I've reread the scriptures looking for guidance as a parent, I have found very few scriptural references dealing with teenagers. Counsel to parents always includes the word *child* or *children:* "Train up a *child* in the way he should go . . ." "Provoke not your *children* to wrath . . ." "And again, inasmuch as parents have *children* in Zion . . ." "And they shall also teach their *children* to pray, and to walk uprightly . . ." (Proverbs 22:6; Ephesians 6:4; D&C 68:25,28; italics added.) References to teenagers are limited to autonomous activities separate from parental jurisdiction: Christ in the temple at age twelve, the prodigal son, Alma's son and the four sons of Mosiah, the stripling warriors, Laman and Lemuel, Samson, and so forth. Such accounts do not reveal much about family structure; rather, they suggest that these young people acted on their own and that parents could only watch and pray. Most scriptural counsel for parents concerns children under twelve, or even under eight.

When a distraught parent of a teenager comes in for help, one of the first things I do is ask questions about the son or daughter's childhood. How often was he or she left with a baby sitter? What kind of health problems did he or she encounter? How is the family structured? What kind of relationship does the wife have with the husband? Having asked these questions for twenty years, I can usually guess the answers from a teen's behavior.

It is surprising, however, to hear teenagers themselves describe what they think their parents should have done during their younger years. The response is remarkably uniform regardless of religion, sex, race, or economic circumstances: more rules, more time spent with parents, family meals and recreation, schedules they can count on. These teenagers talk about the future and what it's going to be like for them: no divorce *no matter what*, much more time spent with *their* children. Teens are often ashamed of their parents, bitter, resentful, and hurt. They feel uncared for, unloved, and therefore unlovable. Even worse, their lack of self-esteem carries over into their adult lives: when selections are made for employment, college, and marriage partners, these unlucky people are often at the bottom of the heap.

Of course, those I see in my work as a psychologist are extreme. But what disturbs me just as much are those teens who live barely above the line. They don't do anything that would land them in my office, but I see them tucking tobacco chews in their back pockets, discussing the latest R-rated movie, laughing at questionable stories, poring over pornographic magazines, packing into cars during their lunch hour and wheeling wildly away and then frequently returning late. Their grades are mediocre and their elective choices follow the line of least resistance. They are seen holding hands on campus at age twelve, intimately swaying in dark corners at unsupervised junior high dances. Parents confide in tired voices how glad they'll be when the teenage years pass. Teachers talk endlessly about the latest technique for controlling disinterested and sometimes rude teenagers, and their own family life is disrupted as they try to be pseudoparents to these frustrated teens.

I've seen even the best teens agonize at age thirteen that they don't have a boyfriend, that they don't have even one pair of designer jeans, that they weren't picked for the team, that their complexions are beyond hope, that the popular kids at school exclude them, that they are overweight or underweight, overdeveloped or underdeveloped. They fret over unfair treatment: everybody else in the neighborhood has a motorcycle, never has to do any chores, gets to shop at the most exclusive stores, has a personal charge card and set of car keys, and has a pocketful of tokens and endless hours to spend at the arcade.

Could training at home have made a difference? When does training turn into unrighteous dominion? At what age do you resign yourself to saying, "Well, they have their free agency"? When should teens no longer be held accountable to you for what they do? Who makes the rules, and what happens when they are broken? Can parents be too strict? What do you do when a teen resists all of the parents' honest efforts?

Would my own young children someday pass this way? What could I do to minimize their problems? My Church callings had made me aware of the Lord's expectations of the youth. As an admissions advisor for the Church Education System I knew the requirements for post-high-school education and the necessity to start preparing as early as possible. I was acquainted with college entrance tests and could see that with rapid Church growth and rising educational costs, requirements for entering LDS schools would be raised higher and higher, and only those fully prepared would qualify. Would my children be among them?

I asked myself these questions, and I heard them from both parents and teenagers I worked with every day. I observed that both parents and teens really wanted to be close. Parents dreamed of the day when their son or daughter would move into the world to make a difference—happy, in love, prepared to live a provident and useful life. Teens wanted their parents' approval, admiration, unconditional love, and trust. They wanted desperately to succeed and to make their loved ones proud.

When President David O. McKay said that no other success can compensate for failure in the home, he confirmed what I saw on the faces of countless parents and teens daily. Neon couldn't flash a brighter message than do the faces of happy parents. And no one looks more dejected than teens and parents in conflict with each other.

Is it important that both win? The Lord said, "This is my work and my glory—to bring to pass the immortality and eternal life of man." (Moses 1:39.) To accomplish this he needs a righteous generation, youth who have discovered that living correctly—which includes honoring their fathers and mothers—frees them to receive all that the Father has. He needs a generation that chooses obedience because it makes life more successful, more uplifting, more progressive. The Lord also needs righteous parents to witness for him. When we account to him for our parental stewardships, will he call our children to testify?

I don't think the Lord will evaluate our success or failure as parents by counting our children's virtues and mistakes. Rather, I think he will be more interested in how hard we tried. He will want to know how important our children were to us and whether our efforts with them were righteous. He has not left us without guidelines—ancient and modern scriptures and prophets and the Holy Ghost (D&C 121:26)—to help us fulfill our stewardship successfully.

I have a hunch the Lord will ask my son Steven how well he handled his trials in life—even if some of them were his parents. I believe he will expect Steven to succeed in spite of unfavorable circumstances. As for me, he will judge my parenthood by his own. The actions of my children won't convict or exalt me, but how I handled their actions will. That is the test of godhood.

It has become clear to me that the role of a parent must be that of a teacher. As Joseph Smith said, "I teach them correct principles and they govern themselves." Your teens will have a head start if they are given experiences that will build their resolve to resist temptation. Telling isn't teaching, and listening isn't learning. The real lessons are learned through experience. (See Alma 32.) Parents are in the best position to provide such experience. I ponder daily: David seems extra tired; I wonder why? Connie has a twinkle in her eye; who put it there? What kind of academic experience does Steven need? How can I motivate him to try harder?

This book is a glimpse into what Sherri and I have learned from our search for answers, and a personal testimony of the value of those principles. As I've prayed for each of my children and asked the Lord what Sherri and I could do to help them learn good from evil, to make choices to live worthily, I have learned and taught these principles.

I caution parents to pray diligently before trying any of the methods in this book. I share them only to show that the Lord will help us tailor our teaching to each individual for whom he has called us to be responsible. As I asked him how to effectively lead my children, I found that the quality I most needed was strong personal discipline. To the extent that I actually did, day in and day out, what I felt inspired to do, I was able to help my children bypass many mistakes and emerge as valiant, righteous disciples of Christ, motivated from within.

Our three daughters are college age. Our two sons are teenagers. It took—and takes—a lot of time. It gave—and gives—unending rewards.

2

The Preteen Years

As a psychologist, I'm constantly asked how to correct misbehavior: What should I do when my children refuse to go to church? What do I do with my son when he takes the car without permission? How can I get my daughter to come in by the curfew? When a parent explains, I can generally see why the child misbehaved, and between the two of us we can speculate on ways to handle the problem. But, curiously, in the most successful families I know, the parents spend their best time and thought not correcting but preventing misbehavior. I've discovered in the course of my lifetime that the best kind of control is self-control. If parents have laid a foundation from the beginning, they may never have to deal with the most serious teenage crises.

To discipline is to instruct, educate, train. Self-control must be taught and nurtured, the earlier the better. A child has to learn what is permissible step by step, over years of experience. A disciplined person voluntarily chooses a certain way of life. If parents themselves have accepted this way of life, then they can help their children develop self-discipline, not by punishing, but by showing, modeling, explaining, and teaching.

Thinking of ourselves as teachers and trainers instead of disciplinarians (though the term still applies, and correctly so) helped my wife and me to see our role a little clearer. Together, we came up with a set of principles we felt applied under this definition:

1. Training begins at birth; however, the child's age and maturity will influence the *kind* of training he or she should receive.

2. An effective teacher-trainer must convey to the child a sure sense of direction. Children like and need structure, despite their sulking, pouting, tantrums, and other ways of testing their parents. What makes a child thrive physically and socially are adult-decided responsibilities, which are gradually given over to the child as he shows himself capable of handling them.

3. Train children in love by helping them repeat acceptable behavior and by lovingly restraining them, if necessary, from repeating unacceptable behavior.

4. Allow your children to talk out their feelings, fears, and frustrations, and to ask such questions as why, what, who, and what for.

5. Mother and father must agree on all issues of principle: religion, curfew, schooling, dating, and so on. Both need to be consistent and persistent.

6. Be in constant communication with your Father in heaven and learn to trust your instincts.

With these guidelines in mind, let's build a foundation for self-discipline, progressing upward by age and stage. Even though we all have children in different stages of development, it helps to take a panoramic view of where children are in the process. If you can see the end from the beginning, you will be better able to evaluate where a gap in training might have occurred and thus take remedial steps where possible.

Self-Centered

During this stage a child depends on others for basic needs, is relatively unprejudiced toward others, acts on his own wishes and needs, and expresses all feelings. Play is an all-consuming concern, and peer pressure has very little influence.

This stage begins at birth and usually phases out around age five or six, when the child leaves the parents' side for extra training by schools, music teachers, coaches, and other adults.

It is important at this age that he receive a lot of attention and direction from parents. You set parameters and provide a daily routine within those parameters. Now is the time to determine what your children will need to know when they leave your side as independent adults.

At this stage children need daily eye contact, touch, hugs, smiles, soft voices, and a comfortable feeling of health from proper feeding and care. Give them plenty of room to grow and learn. Make your home safe for them. If they move toward danger or trouble, intervene with another activity. Introduce them hourly to their new world; stimulate their senses. Let them know that *you* make their life happy.

When your child bites, don't bite back to show how much it hurts. At this stage children aren't capable of transferring learning. Find something he *can* bite and move him away from the situation that prompted the problem biting. Use eye contact every time you are specifically training the child, and speak in the tone of voice you wish him to use.

Between three and five years of age, a child should learn to care for himself and the home. Remember, he must be walked with every step of the way—say, "This is what grown-ups do!" Use the word *let's*: "Let's brush your teeth. Let's make your bed. Let's pick up the toys. Let's set the table. Let's take your bath." Set the routine. Your child will learn faster if it's repeated day after day with you right by his side.

Hug a lot. Explain everything. Avoid don'ts. Praise efforts: "I like the way you remembered to put the lid back on the toothpaste." "You are learning to sit quietly during church just like Daddy." Be positive: "You can do it!" "You are special!" "You are wonderful!" "You are growing up!"

Skill-Centered

At this stage, about ages six to twelve, conflict arises between the need for guidance and the need for independence. Your child will begin to discover new values and to question old ones.

The arrival of this stage indicates that a significant amount of teaching and learning has already taken place and that your child is anxious to do and think for himself. Disciplining with logical consequences will best teach a healthy sense of independence.

You'll know when your child reaches this stage. You will be helping him make his bed and he will suddenly look up and say, "I can do it all by myself." Then, for the next several years, it will be trial and error. Your child will want to go it alone and will be frustrated at any inability to do things up to standard. He will know what to do and will not want you to tell him to do it—even when he forgets or does it poorly. So this is the time to stay close by and help with subtlety.

As the parent, you will still set the parameters, but now the child can help you plan the daily routine. Six- to nine-year-olds need lots of opportunities to make simple choices (out of several alternatives that would be acceptable to you). List activities, chores, responsibilities, and rules; then let your child help choose how these will be carried out. Keep the chores few and simple so you can check on them consistently. Make your child feel you depend on him.

Continue to walk with him, if necessary, to see that he accomplishes what he agreed to do. Give small, tangible rewards *after* a job well done—never to stop undesirable behavior. Hug him, talk to him eye to eye, feed him well, keep him comfortably dressed, and smile when you look at him.

Between ages ten and twelve children do not like to be

told what to do, so use a chart. Again, make a list together, including the times when tasks should be accomplished. Hold your son or daughter to it through natural consequences. For instance, he doesn't leave the house in the morning till the chores are done; he doesn't go to bed until chores are done. Children need to experience the grown-up feeling of receiving privileges by earning them.

Be positive, matter-of-fact, and honest. Let the chart tell the child what he's earned. Love, support, and guide him, but don't take away the consequences, or you will be teaching him to misbehave again. Keep touching; sit together, hug, or rub a tired back.

Provide adventures together and times for serious talks when your child can pour out thoughts, feelings, fears, and frustrations without feeling threatened. This will create a habit that will carry over into the teen years, easing the way for healthy communication later on.

Help your child choose at least two areas to excel in, and help him form good study habits *now*. Conquering a difficult subject or learning to play an instrument or a sport well is hard. Your child will make hundreds of mistakes. When your child grows resistant—no one likes to fail—you need to be the strong one, giving emotional support and encouragement but holding your child to practice or study. Without this firm support, a child will back away from the struggle and remain on the level at which he feels competent.

Don't be swayed by your child's excuses. Knowing the mitigating circumstances may help you evaluate how to correct misbehavior—but such circumstances do not and should not remove the consequences.

Service-Centered

When children reach this stage, their first concern is for others. They are able to nurture others without sacrificing personal growth. They know the right reasons for giving, have a positive self-image, and take responsibility for providing their own physical, financial, and emotional needs. Such people are self-motivated and self-actualized; they work toward achieving their own potential. And they are able to establish and maintain harmony with the laws of God and society, knowing that their own strength comes through obedience to these laws. The rewards are freedom, self-respect, and the respect of others. When a child has arrived at this stage, you will know he is well on his way to reaching his potential.

Between ages thirteen and sixteen, if the child has lived within a clear set of parameters, he plans his own daily routine and sets goals. You are still very much available; you meet with your teen and plan ahead through daily conversations and weekly planning sessions.

Clearly define what you expect, and then let him schedule himself to meet those expectations. Have him make a list of Musts, Oughts, and Wants. Then ask him to arrange these things in a workable schedule and present it to you; this will help you work together, not interfering with one another's goals. It should be clearly understood that your teen has privileges (not rights) that are granted according to mature behavior and concern for the rights and privileges of others.

Your role as an authority will be paramount when your teen needs to fall back on it to save face with his peers. Peer interaction reaches its peak in most teenagers when they reach fifteen years old. That is the time to stay close and be there to support them. Teens need a chance to test and evaluate principles at home with support from those who love them—even when they occasionally fall.

Our son David was encouraged by a neighbor friend to set fire to some explosives. He sensed that we would not approve, so he took the precaution of keeping the plan a secret. When an explosion damaged his left hand severely, it took a great deal of courage for him to admit that he had done something foolish. But the pain and fear of losing his hand left him no choice.

The doctor diagnosed burned tendons. David would need surgery. His hand would also be scarred to the point of needing plastic surgery. David asked me for a blessing. With our home teacher, Wayne Whitlock, assisting me, I felt impressed to bless David that his hand would heal without scars. The next day when the doctor removed the bandages to prepare for surgery, David's hand had visibly improved. Within a very short time it was completely healed, with no visible sign of the mishap.

The experience left David with mixed emotions: a feeling of awe for the power of the priesthood, a healthy respect for explosives, gratitude for his reprieve, and the knowledge that repeated disobedience could place him outside his covenant relationship with the Lord in the future.

Between ages sixteen and nineteen, teens can learn to provide for themselves financially. They need to feel competent, successful, useful, and important. They need monitored exposure to reality with time to evaluate and analyze how they respond. This is the age for driver's licenses, dating, and plans that will take them away from home.

These teens still see you as the authority in your home. If you neglect to follow through on limits, they learn that authority can be challenged when it interferes with their immediate desires. They want the security of limits. They need to understand that freedom brings responsibilities and that they have an obligation to pay their own way in life. Your teens will accept these principles happily if you have prepared them during the earlier stages of development.

Let's use the money issue as an example. Sherri and I make sure our teenagers know that they live in *our* home and use *our* car. Therefore, we make the rules governing the home and the use of the car. We explain that someday they will have their own possessions. They don't have to account to us for what they do with their belongings—only for what they do with ours.

This has encouraged our children to search for ways to acquire the things they want. Our eldest daughter, Kathy, took many things into her marriage that would make a home comfortable, including lovely paintings and wall hangings, several pieces of furniture she had refinished herself, and a large trousseau. Carolyn, Connie, David, and Steven are following in her footsteps.

As our children turn sixteen, we turn the household budget over to them for the summer. They pay utilities, buy the food, plan the menus, feed us three meals a day, budget for gas, and meet other necessities. We find *them* reminding *us* to keep the door closed so the air conditioner won't be required to cool the entire outdoors. They struggle when there is too much month at the end of the money and burst into tears when the dessert is sampled early. The accounting at the end of each month is an especially valuable lesson.

Sherri loves to sew and makes a considerable amount of what we wear. But she had to struggle with each of our daughters to teach them the skill. It was interesting, though, that when Kathy married, she asked to borrow the old sewing machine we had in storage. With that machine, she made her curtains, maternity clothes, baby clothes, slipcovers, aprons, baby toys, and gifts. She also keeps her family healthy, grinding her own wheat and making bread, gleaning from orchards and gardens, canning and drying. Her ability to manage the small income of a student husband helped keep him in college. She is using the lessons learned at home, lessons that were sometimes hard to teach her.

We take self-sufficiency seriously. All our sons and daughters have learned how to bake bread, sew, clean, and choose and care for their clothes. When they turn twelve, they take over their own washing and ironing. Fifteen-year-old David sorts a wash, adds the detergent, knows when to add bleach, and irons his own white shirt for Sunday.

There's a certain virtue in working hard as well as working skillfully. Our farm gave hundreds of opportunities—changing water; milking the cow; weeding; picking and selling fruit from our fruit trees; canning, drying, and preserving food. When we moved to the city, we switched to painting house numbers on curbs; making suckers and selling them at football games; giving piano, violin, and gymnastics lessons to the children in the neighborhood; baby-sitting; and eventually applying for jobs and working hard to keep them.

We let our children know they were responsible for taking the driver's education course before driving and that they had to earn good grades to keep the insurance cost down. We told them one ticket would cost them a three-month suspension of their license, the second six months, and the third, suspension for a year. We established our right to know where they were going with the car and when they planned to return. When they have announced, "I can earn the money to buy my own car," we have counterannounced that they will also need to earn enough to support themselves too. This does not mean that they would have to leave home to get a car—just that a car is definitely a luxury and a low priority.

We thought through and talked through these issues before our eldest could drive, so our children grew up knowing the family's rules. We had observed that cars create a false sense of independence and also cost a great deal of money. We didn't want our teens, in their immaturity, to liquidate college tuition savings in order to pay for a car. Much of what we did, frankly, postponed decisions about cars until they were mature enough that a car fit into—instead of dominated—their lives.

On the other hand, we have been very open to their responsible use of our cars. They have all found quality jobs that have helped them to finance their needs, including the gas they use. We continue to give gifts that we hope are both generous and sensitive, but from age sixteen on our children have earned their necessities completely, including putting themselves through college full-time. We've helped when it was needed (for instance, contributing large amounts toward tuition), but generally they meet their needs through their own efforts. Their confidence has grown as they have felt competent and useful. By gaining and honing marketable skills, they are able to face their futures with equanimity.

We found it was unnecessary to ground or otherwise punish our children at this age. Indeed, we have found that there is very little you can really do to discipline teenagers, since they are physically able to do just about anything they want to do. Thus, it is imperative that they control themselves. They no longer need someone right by their side but can be completely independent so long as they control their behavior. With independence comes responsibility; if they choose to behave correctly, they receive the reward they have earned. If they use their freedom incorrectly, then they must assume the consequences, which may include restrictions. We have tried to make it very clear to our children that they can choose to be controlled or to control themselves. The latter is the apex of true freedom.

We cannot expect our children to do more or less than they are able. To become capable they first need to be taught and trained, then given opportunities to do things alone with us close by, and then—on their own—take responsibility for their actions.

It takes a dispassionate parent to analyze the beginning with the end in mind, to allow children to progress past the self-centered stage and to assume supervised independence that becomes self-motivated independence. If children can be taught to direct themselves before they leave home, they will be capable of living independently. They will be free, responsible, righteous adults, our peers as well as our children. What more, as parents, could we desire?

3

The Teen Years

What if those preteen years have slipped away and the teen has not yet learned to be responsible?

"There is no way my teen could possibly hold down a job at sixteen—he can't even follow through on one task I give him here at home to do. He flaunts my curfew rules, is failing in school, hasn't developed any talents, and hangs around with a group of teenagers I don't approve of. The thought of sitting down together and working on goals is unthinkable. He doesn't even eat with us at the table, let alone join us for a planning session."

"My daughter has been dating since thirteen and is going steady at fifteen. If I tried to break them up, I believe she would run away."

In my work as a school psychologist, I hear these comments often, from parents sometimes bitter, sometimes despairing. Included are the tragic stories of drugs, promiscuity, theft, even homicide and suicide.

I have sensed feelings of guilt and resentment when I've sketched the scenario in the preceding chapter. The gap between what should have been done years ago and what actually took place can leave a feeling of helplessness and failure. "But what can I do *now*? Is it too late?"

The answer is no. I truly believe that it is never too late, even after death. And the first step in changing things is to get rid of that sense of failure. Not only does it paralyze your own sense of direction ("If it's too late, there's nothing I can do now"), but your teen may sense that feeling and transfer it to himself. You may nonverbally communicate such thoughts as:

"You're worthless now—ruined. Why try anymore? You're never going to amount to anything. I'm tired of trying. I don't want any more to do with you." I've even heard parents compare their life with the war in heaven: "God lost a third of his spirit children!" In effect, such parents are throwing away their children.

Take away a person's belief in himself and emphasize that no one else believes in him either, and what do you have left? A person in this state of mind will react one of three ways: (1) something inside him will fight and search for someone or something to restore a sense of worth; (2) he will withdraw from challenge *and* from failure; or (3) he will entertain thoughts of ending his life. If he chooses the first, the search, he has two choices—he could get involved in drugs, promiscuity, gambling, theft, and other antisocial activities, or he could rise through his own determination to prove everyone wrong. Many success stories recount the triumphant struggle with a deprived childhood that motivated a youth to change his circumstances by changing his life.

The most common reaction to feelings of failure, however, and the one least noticed by adults, is choosing to be mediocre—choosing the line of least resistance; doing just enough to keep out of real trouble. Children who take this course stop wanting to be or do anything really significant.

What can parents do? The hardest work is to keep things in perspective. Because of our children's premortal existence, they, like us, come into life with unique personalities and already-developed character traits. You don't get a manufacturer's handbook, though, with a child, so beware of simply blaming things you don't like on the preexistence. Heredity also adds thousands of physical variables that will determine in part his capacity for growth and opportunities. These are givens. Your children are stuck with yours just as you're stuck with theirs.

Environment, the third major influence, is where you

have your influence. Yet others also have influence in this area. Sometimes, through no fault of the parents, someone may have given a teen a view of reality that the parents don't agree with. For years our daughter looked forward to college, took college prep courses, planned on a degree, and looked forward to marriage and a home and family. Then, right in the middle of a discussion with me about the future, she burst into tears and said, "All this planning is pointless. There's no point in talking about it anymore."

I was horrified. She had sacrificed many teenage parties and frivolous activities for Church service and disciplined study. What had happened? A few questions revealed a discussion she had had with an influential Church leader who had speculated casually about the approximate date of the great conflicts preceding the second coming of Christ. He felt the date for a holocaust could be as early as 1986. This fear, perhaps coupled with rumors at school and media concern about nuclear weapons, paralyzed her. "I may not even be here by then," she wailed. "Why should I prepare for something that may not even happen?" Preparation now seemed like a waste of time.

Sherri and I explained that we had entertained the same fears and showed her some of the debate notes we had used in college about the arms race and impending holocaust. We were still here, even though we couldn't guarantee her tomorrow. She listened as we counseled her to make her plans as though she were going to live a hundred years.

The next day she filled out her application for college—something she had put off for months.

What if we had not had the discussion? What if our daughter's environment had continued to be shaped by that one experience? How many teenagers are there who just need someone to talk to?

What can a parent do? Start by having a heart-to-heart talk with a teenager who has started to stray—or, indeed, one who has been straying. The relationship between you needs to be one of love and trust. In fact, if you aren't close enough to talk openly and honestly, it may be an indication that your teen is doing something he knows you wouldn't like. If my teen fails to look me in the eye when we are talking, or is evasive or vague, I know it's time to have a heart-to-heart interview without fail and without delay.

During such interviews, I don't demand that my teen open up, but I do ask, "Is there anything on your mind I need to know about? Something seems to be bothering you. If so, I'd like to help."

If he insists everything is all right and I can sense it is not, I smile at him warmly and thank him for talking with me. I make it clear that I'm available if there is anything he needs help with in the future.

Then I return to step one, the self-centered stage, as mentioned in chapter 2. How is this done with a teenager? Read his needs and meet them promptly, exactly as you did when he was a baby. Find every excuse you can think of to be with him. Attend his activities, work with him while he is doing his chores, fix his favorite foods, find everything you can that's good about him and tell him often. Step up the physical affection. And pray. Pray to feel love overriding your anger and disappointment. Pray for patience. Pray for sensitivity about the teen's needs. Your teen probably isn't praying very much—you pray for him.

But isn't this approach just abandoning standards, discipline, and responsibility—showing the other children that they can get away with anything? No, it isn't, because along with the love, you also go back to early discipline.

When you are interacting with a newborn, you don't expect very much from him. You take care of his needs, you keep him close to you, and you cuddle him continuously. If, as a baby, he picks up a knife, you don't give him a long discourse on why knives are dangerous and should not be one of his playthings. You divert his attention to something he can play with and place the knife in a place where he can't reach it.

When a relationship needs to be rekindled, that isn't the time to preach or nag or point out what the person is doing wrong. Teenagers almost always know when they are doing something wrong—but, like a newborn, they have little personal control and need support to regain the strength to overcome their problems. As with a baby, that means making the environment safe again. Of course, it's harder with a teen because you don't have complete control over his environment.

Remember, you accept your child, but you don't accept his behavior. Your teen needs to understand that he must earn the freedom to direct his own life. If the relationship between the two of you has deteriorated to the point that he is destructive physically, mentally, or spiritually, then he may have to be removed for a time to prevent him from repeating transgressions that would double his recovery time. Consult professionals. Pretending the problem doesn't exist, refusing to face it, backing down from dealing with it—these approaches are extremely damaging, both to your relationship and to your teen's opportunities to progress.

I remember a teenage friend whose father was the stake president. Because his father rarely spent time with him, he drifted into a group that satisfied his need to belong. Cigarettes were part of their life-style. He accepted them and, before long, had become addicted. But he hated himself for it and desperately wanted to quit. Lacking the strength to tell his friends no, he needed the strength of his parents to "forbid" him to see these friends again. So he placed a package of cigarettes in his coat pocket and left the coat in the front hall with the package of cigarettes showing. He told me how he watched from an adjoining room as his father walked in the front door—praying that his father would see the cigarettes and call him to task. He said his father immediately saw the coat, stopped short as his eyes fell on the cigarettes, pulled them from the pocket and looked at them with a shocked, hurt look, shook his head, and replaced the cigarettes in the pocket. My friend said he waited for the deserved rebuke, but his father, not knowing how to handle the situation, did nothing. He had to leave for another meeting and kept postponing the confrontation until he knew what to say. The time never came. The young man felt betrayed, rejected, and uncared for. He continued to flounder.

In this young teen's case, a clear requirement that he leave the cigarettes alone was what the young man wanted—removing the knife. Then he needed a more attractive diversion—a man-to-man talk about the future, preparing for it, outlining steps toward it, with the parent defining the parameters for him for a while.

A teenager on drugs requires the same firm control, with the parent available constantly to help him overcome the habit. The teenager needs the daily support of encouraging, loving words: "You can overcome this, and you must. You have too much to offer in this life, many great things to accomplish. You're needed, you're important, you're special, and I just can't stand by and watch you give up everything without a fight."

You need to pray with all of your soul to be able to say that and mean it. Nagging, forcing, and intimidation are all negative influences that hinder the communication of love and, inevitably, the ability to influence. It is vital, therefore, to communicate in every way you can that you love your child unconditionally. He needs to understand that it is his behavior that needs changing—not him personally—and not for *you* personally. Forget about any embarrassment you might be feeling because you have a son or daughter in trouble. Focus on your vision for your children and your desire to help them overcome any obstacle that would curtail their full enjoyment of life.

I remember a family that communicated this beautifully. The parents were active in the Church, had several children, and had worked diligently to teach them the gospel. However, one of their daughters, a beautiful, queenly girl, began sampling life with a group who did not live up to her standards. She began accepting drinks at parties, and one thing led to another. Before long, she became pregnant. She said that her first thoughts were mercilessly accusing: "You're worthless now. Ruined. Why try anymore? No good man is going to want you. Enjoy life while you can. Drop out of school. You're not going to need an education anymore. Keep your baby and teach her that life is unfair and cruel and that the only way to survive is to look out for number one. Don't provide her with a father. Teach her to hate men. You're not worthy to attend Church anymore. Stay away from the bishop. He'll only use you as an example to the other girls of how not to be. You don't need that. Come to the singles bar where you can really be appreciated. There is work for you there, money to be made, great times still ahead."

Her wonderful parents, however, convinced her that she had everything in life to look forward to. They counseled her to go to the bishop and do whatever he told her to do—that they loved her and would support her through it. The bishop counseled her to give up the baby for adoption and go back to school. She did, though it took two years before she felt really worthy to attend church without feeling the sting of guilt. She hardly trusted herself in any situation and even felt hesitant about accepting dates with worthy returned missionaries. But she kept diligently to her studies, and eventually, just before graduating from college, she met a persistent young man who saw her and loved her. Today, they have a lovely family, he's a doctor and a member of the bishopric; she's on the Relief Society stake board. Their eldest son is on a mission, and their daughter was just married in the temple. Here was a teen who, through the support of her family, was able to believe in herself again, and her life returned to its progressive course.

The kind of trouble a teen can attract can have lifelong consequences. It is vital that someone reach out—and it may take more than one person. It may be a Scoutmaster, a seminary teacher, a truant officer, an aunt, or a grandparent. When a teen feels guilty and aware of transgression, he may not believe it when someone tells him he is still worthwhile. He may need several to provide that witness to him.

Change never happens without a price, and your teen may not have what it takes. Can you pay that price in money, time, prayers, and an unyielding faith in him when all his faith in himself is gone?

Your teen will need individual contact daily with someone to whom he or she accounts for his or her behavior and who provides opportunities to overcome the problem: repay the shoplifting, place the baby for adoption, turn oneself in for drug rehabilitation. This person must also help the teen refocus on the future with a new vision.

The troubled teen needs a lot of opportunities to talk about his feelings, fears, and worries. He needs someone he can go to when he feels as though he's slipping again, someone who will help him be strong until the urge passes.

Then he needs to begin building for the future by developing a talent or a skill. One of the 1984 Olympic skiers is a former juvenile delinquent whose therapy required him to develop a talent. In a tightly structured daily routine, he perfected his talent.

What if your teen rejects you, won't talk, runs away, gets institutionalized? Or just quits school, leaves town, or sets up in an apartment of his own? What if he won't meet with you, hangs up on phone calls, or tears up letters? What if you're reaching but he's beyond reach? Remember, he isn't.

Never, never, never give up. Don't give up your love for him. Don't give up your vision for him. Don't give up his place in the family circle.

What you can do is continue to provide a firm witness of what is right, your faith in your teen's ability to discipline himself, and your equally firm witness that he has greatness in him. What you can't control is your teen's behavior. What you *can* control, with the Lord's help, is yours. And that includes setting standards for your teen and requiring accountability.

One young teenage girl insisted on courting the favors of a young man who persistently encouraged her to go against her standards. He tempted her with marijuana and succeeded. When she became pregnant, he helped her get an abortion. All efforts of the parents to stop their daughter from seeing him failed. They finally told her she would have to choose between seeing the young man or living in their home. Marijuana would no longer be tolerated in the house, nor would the presence of the young man. She chose to leave home.

As they watched her pack her belongings, they told her they wanted her to know two things. First, no matter what she did, they would always love her. Second, they said "You are our daughter and we will never deny that relationship."

She disappeared for some time—communicating with her elder brother now and then, but refusing to have anything to do with her parents.

The family prayed for her daily and expressed a continual desire for her welfare. The daughter, meanwhile, lived the life she wanted to live. It seemed okay for a while, but in her heart she learned to understand what her parents had against the things she was doing. She began to realize how unfair it was of her to expect her parents to have to pick up the pieces time after time while she flaunted their rules.

When left alone to live as she chose, she suddenly realized that her life's direction truly was her decision. Was this what she *really* wanted? Did she enjoy the freedoms that were slowly enslaving her? What did she really believe in? What did she want out of life? The moment of decision for her came when she faced a second pregnancy. She had quickly removed the inconvenience before under the direction of her boyfriend. But would she go through it again? She decided it was time to make decisions on her own.

Deciding that abortion was wrong and making the decision to have the baby, she now faced the question of where to go from there. To stay in the environment she was in would only compound her problems. No one was willing to support her righteous desires.

Wanting the best for her unborn baby, she suddenly understood the unconditional love for her that her parents had expressed the night she left home. Mustering courage, she humbly rang the doorbell of her parents' home. They were there—physically, emotionally, and spiritually. She understood the conditions of her remaining there and accepted her parents' right to require them. With their help she was able to slowly regain the strength she needed to cope independently.

The parents were careful to convey to their daughter in every way they could that *they* were not her source of strength. She would become strong by accepting responsibility for her actions and living in accordance with correct principles.

They lovingly pointed out that, though their love would never wane, it could not magically remove the effects of drug addiction or the reality of pregnancy. What their love could accomplish was to provide an outstretched hand to pull their teen back onto the straight and narrow way—if that was where she chose to go.

They did not succumb to the temptation to relive the past. Though they knew there may have been times when they hadn't done all they thought they should have in those preteen years, they refused to let their teen communicate to them such false messages as "It's too late" or "This is all your fault." They understood that she would have to answer for her life regardless of what they did or didn't do. She had her agency and so did they. The thing to do now was to concentrate on the best possible future.

Contrasting examples include the mother whose son has weathered a divorce and committed criminal acts. She has paid his fines, fed him, cared for his children, bought his cars, and bailed him out when he's lost job after job. Afraid to stand up to him for fear of having him run away, she has bent to his demands, allowed her home to be filled with black-painted walls; strobe lights; loud, pulsating music; and marijuana smoke. "He's my son and I love him; I can't bear to see him go without," she says.

Another mother whose son has committed similar errors counseled him to find a way to pay his bills or suffer the consequences. She has continued with her life of service as a temple worker, has completed two missions for the Church, and sends her love consistently through letters and gifts to him as to her other children. "I love him dearly," she commented, "and pray for the day when he will remember who and what he is and rise to it!"

Remember, it is not the actions of our children that will determine the quality of our parenting. How we handle those actions is what counts. I'll never forget the time we gave two of our children, ages thirteen and nine, some money to spend at a nearby mall. They brought home a pocketful of penny candy to share with the rest of the family. A week later, they wanted to do it again with their allowance, so we took them to the mall and gave them instructions to meet us at the front of the mall in an hour. No sooner had we arrived home than the telephone rang.

"Hello, may I speak to the Zirkers, please? Two of your children tried to walk out of my restaurant without paying for their dinner. I would appreciate it if you could come down immediately and take care of this matter."

Sherri's best friend happened to be at the house when the telephone call came. She had wanted children of her own for years and had frequently told us how she envied our family life. We were doubly embarrassed at the less-than-exemplary stunt.

Excusing ourselves, we went to the mall, paid the bill, and had a serious discussion all the way home. Children who take what isn't theirs have to be watched, we told them, so they could not be alone in public. There were several opportunities available at home to work off the amount we had paid for them, and the minute they arrived home would be a good time to start. Children who wouldn't control their behavior also couldn't enjoy privileges reserved for those who would.

Several weeks later, Sherri's friend telephoned to talk about the experience and surprised her by saying, "I never envied your parenthood as much as I did that day."

"You've got to be kidding," Sherri said. "It wasn't exactly my most uplifting experience."

"No," her friend continued, "you had the privilege that day of communicating a great lesson to your children. Who else would take the time to monitor their behavior and teach them a better way? You were needed and you were available. You're in the position of being the greatest influence they have. Oh, Sherri, do you know how blessed you are?"

That friend gave us a new perspective. Besides giving troubled children time and attention, we need to demonstrate the tough kind of love that communicates, "You are too important to be allowed to believe that blessings can be obtained without paying a price for them." Parents also need to communicate the steps involved in paying the price, walking children through restitution, standing by them during—but not shielding them from—consequences.

Teens need to understand that repentance is the tool

that removes them from the influence of the adversary and restores their ability to progress under the influence of the Holy Ghost. Sometimes, this experience with the contrast in feelings and self-evaluation is one of the best teachers of values there is.

After all, the only control that counts in the eyes of the Lord is self-control. Your goal isn't to gain control over your teen so he won't transgress anymore, but to help him want control for himself—not to save you embarrassment, but because you know he will be happier.

If your teen is still in the house and under your influence, do something drastic to alter the environment. A day—or better yet, a week—away backpacking, horseback riding, or canoeing is great. This time should be spent in a place where the influences of the world are minimized and your awareness of each other is maximized. It is not the time for preaching. You may not even say a word. Certainly, parts of the experience will be awkward if you have drifted apart. Be prepared for that. Also be ready to see and share humor in your situation. Laughter is a great bond. Change takes place only after a significant emotional experience. You need to provide a setting where love can reassert its force.

This is also a time for you to do some rethinking and refeeling. Don't be discouraged if nothing magic happens. The simple fact that you have chosen to spend time with your teen is a powerful message. Choose the same course again and again, if necessary, until he believes that love is behind the choice.

With love comes discipline. Don't expect cooperation in the beginning, but do require obedience. Set the requirements and insist on accountability. (If you don't do this, a truant officer will, or a bishop, or a juvenile court.) You are not bargaining with your teen, bribing him, punishing him, or threatening him. He is free to accept or reject the conditions of remaining in your home, eating the food you purchase, and wearing the clothes you buy. Freedom must be earned by responsible behavior, nothing more, nothing less. It is a hard lesson to learn—especially for one who has tasted freedom without paying the price. That's why it may take more adults, more witnesses, more help, perhaps even more physical restraints: an institution, even jail. Be sure that you understand clearly the consequences of both obedience and disobedience and are committed to them before you make them clear to your teen. Be sure you explain the rewards of obedience as clearly as you explain the penalties of disobedience. Be sure you are realistic. You cannot require your teen to "gain a testimony." You may not even be able to require your teen to "read the scriptures." You can, however, require him to "take your turn offering family prayer and take your turn reading during family scripture study." And keep the list manageable. Since you are requiring daily accountability, you should deal with a limited number of daily or at least weekly activities.

This period of spelled-out behavior and daily accountability must endure until you know your teen understands the need for restraints. Bishops sometimes set tentative timetables—a year of clean living before a temple recommend is issued or reissued. Truant officers let a youth out on probation and still require him to report weekly. Do not give in to either rebellion or sudden sweetness. Bestowing rewards on undeserving teens breeds mediocrity and irresponsibility. He must earn privileges.

However, the requirements and accountability are there, once set up. While he is waiting, and earning, and repaying, and restoring, and restraining—walk with him. Be a companion. Let him cry, and hurt, and talk, and talk, and talk. Rub a tired back, toss him his favorite candy bar, go out for a milk shake, fill a warm bath, keep stew on the burner, ask him to wash the car or to scratch the itch on *your* back.

Through all of your giving and caring and support, keep that vision of future responsibilities and freedoms before your teen. Let him imagine himself in settings where he will be not only able to support himself, but also be capable and prepared to help others. Keep the vision specific with a projected timetable.

And keep praying. Remember, this child is Heavenly Father's, too. You are not alone in your parental concern.

I remember well a case in which a family's continuity for training and teaching their children was broken continually by frequent moves. This often meant changing schools as well as neighborhoods, bishops, ward families, and other supportive help such as nearby relatives.

For some of the children the experience was an adventure, and they thrived on the changes, capitalizing on their ability to meet new people and learn new things.

For one son and one daughter, it was a disaster. Unable to move quickly into a new situation, they were each placed in the same grade two years in a row, were unable to discern the character of certain groups of teenagers, and eventually found themselves in company with those who encouraged them to significantly lower their standards. To further complicate matters, their father, prominent in business and church circles, was gone most of the time, leaving the mother to do most of the counseling and monitoring.

With several children at home and a disposition to mother young people away from home, the mother felt that tight surveillance on this particular problem did not seem warranted. Indeed, the behavior of both the son and the daughter remained mostly unnoticed. The young man began smoking and drinking; the young lady at age twelve began heavily dating men who were several years her senior.

The gap began to widen between the life-styles of these two teens and the accomplishments of those in the family who coped successfully. Repeated references to that effect didn't help to bolster the already diminishing self-esteem of the erring son and daughter.

Conflict in the family increased as the low achievers were pitted against the high achievers. The result was early marriages for the son and daughter in trouble. The girl was married at age fifteen to a young man with questionable attributes. Though he was a member of the Church, he had joined only the year before, hadn't served a mission, and worked with his father as a laborer. The son married a young girl, a junior in high school, the week after he graduated—no college, no job training, no mission.

Though these marriages broke the parents' hearts, they tried to stay close to their children. They invited them to all of the family reunions and planned holiday parties and get-togethers, but the gap widened over the years. The rest of the children graduated from college; married strong, active Church members; and were able to provide stability for the new little spirits they gave birth to. With this stability, the grandchildren in these families grew and developed their talents, learning to serve and love those around them. They were bright students and earned scholarships to college and brought honor to their name.

In the other two homes, lack of stability and intense emotional conflict led to broken marriages, broken hopes, broken lives. The patterns for breaking the Word of Wisdom and the moral code became part of life for the next generation.

In spite of the differences between all of the children, however, a common thread bound them together emotionally and socially. Their parents had taken them on yearly vacations from the time they were born. They shared a common memory of hiking in the woods, swimming in the creek, pitching the tent, building huge bonfires, and singing and telling stories in the pitch-black of the night inside the tent. A deep friendship had developed between the entire family, and the gap closed when these memories surfaced.

Also, the parents had steadily held family prayers from the time they were married and had consistently talked of standards, temple covenants, and the importance of the gospel. Church attendance was automatic. Even when the son and daughter felt most alienated from the family and Church standards, they still felt at home at church.

The time came when bitter words were spoken, and in their own time and their separate circumstances, the son and daughter both moved far away and communication was lost for a time. The sons and daughters who had remained faithful felt "good riddance." They felt their brother and sister were an embarrassment to the family, and there was always an undercurrent of tension when they were around.

Then a conference address by one of the General Authorities pricked their hearts. He talked about repenting and forgiving, and he encouraged more loving and accepting. The righteous sons and daughters searched their hearts for the love and comradeship they had once shared and fanned the dying embers into a burning flame. They purged their souls of the self-righteous disgust they felt when they noticed the ashtrays in their brother's home or the worldliness in their sister's life-style.

They wondered if their bigotry had helped widen the gap—if they had closed doors that their siblings might someday desire to enter. They prayed night and morning with their parents—not just for the members of the family who had strayed, but for the members of the family who lacked compassion, unconditional love, patience, and acceptance. They now prayed to find an opportunity just to let their brother and sister know they loved them.

One daughter remembers taking a week to gain enough courage to call her sister. She hadn't spoken to her for years and was afraid her efforts would be rejected. She decided that she would have faith that the Lord loved them both and would soften her sister's heart.

With a sincere and prayerful heart, she dialed the number. The tears in the voice of her sister were evidence enough that heart had reached heart and spirit had communicated with spirit. Truly sisters once more, they planned a reunion.

Years of animosity were dissolved, bitterness was erased, and the healing began. The family communicated with their brother, and the barriers that had made him feel so worthless began to be removed—more slowly than the sister's, but steadily.

Today, the daughter and her husband are preparing to enter the temple. "For years I have envied you—wanting desperately to have the gospel in my home like you had—wanting a priesthood holder to bless our home and give stability like your husbands did," she told her mother and sisters. For the first time in their married life, her husband was worthy to bless her during a recent illness.

Her own children sensed the change and are now making changes in their own lives. The guarded superficiality and undercurrent of tension is gone—from Church members, from the family within their family, and wholeheartedly from the family they grew up in.

I think the lesson that remains paramount, and one that all parents need to remember, is that regardless of the ages and stages children are in, they all have a common eternal ancestry. Their roots go beyond the stage they missed in their training and monitoring. Inside every child is a divine spirit. If divine principles are used, the spirit has a better-than-average chance to respond. That is why it is so important to pray, ponder, and meditate. We need to consistently seek to hear the word of the Lord.

This principle might tell you to wait for the final score—not to judge too readily. It may tell you to continue to love your children and set a good example. It will also remind you that it is not your responsibility to make your children accept the gospel or love you and all you stand for. You must stop taking the blame and start letting them accept the responsibility for their own actions.

All parents hope that their teens will eventually learn that life is full of problems and that easy solutions are not always available. We cannot avoid pain, frustration, and hard work, but personal growth results from learning to face and overcome difficulties. Parents also hope that youth will learn for themselves that self-reliance and inner motivation are the most important ingredients in successfully meeting life's problems, and that they are personally capable of achieving such success—if not today, surely tomorrow!

4

Traps for Teens

All teenagers dream big about the future. At the same time, they hunger for something here and now—a boyfriend, a position on the football team, a queen's title, a date to the prom, a pair of shoes just like Kyle's, an invitation to join the gang at McDonald's after the game. Two questions to ask teens are: What is it that you want right now more than anything else in the world? Is that consistent with what you want to become?

The way teenagers spend their time is crucial to their future. They will someday look back and either be grateful for the things they learned and applied, or puzzled and upset that they aren't what they want to be. Here are some things that may get in the way of future success:

Carelessness

Our insurance agent stopped by one night. When I let him in, he walked to the nearest chair and slumped down into it. Slowly he shook his head from side to side, and then he began to speak.

His teenage son and a friend were helping a neighboring farmer change water by moving the pipes to another part of the field. Tired of walking the distance, they reasoned that if they raised the pipe in the air and pivoted it in the direction they wanted it to land, they would get the job done quicker. They lifted the pipe right into a high-voltage wire, which electrocuted both of them immediately.

As a student, I remember visiting the dean of my college to give him an update on my progress. As I entered his office I noticed that his face was ashen. He looked as if he was in shock. I waited a moment, giving him time to compose himself.

"My youngest son . . ." he began. The son had brought his buddy up to his room to see his .22 rifle and let him handle it for a moment. Taking the gun in his hand, the friend struck a macho pose, aimed the gun, and pulled the trigger without checking to see whether the gun was loaded or not. "It was. The bullet hit my son in the forehead and killed him instantly."

I loved guns and hunted every year with my dad and my uncles. No one was more excited than I was when I received my first gun—a .22 rifle—for Christmas. I couldn't wait to use it and ran outside, popping off at anything that moved. I hit a bird. Watching it fall to the ground, writhe momentarily, then lie still made me sick inside. I vowed at that moment that I would never again kill for sport.

Teaching carefulness begins with helping toddlers envision consequences: "What will happen if you drop the cup?" It continues with safety instruction—how to respect speed, heat, cold, gravity, explosives, chemicals, and pressures. You can also teach such habits as planning, sizing up, and imagining consequences. Provide many, many, many supervised experiences. Speed, weapons, and chemicals—especially drugs—are so susceptible to misuse among teenagers that they must always be supervised during these years.

Lack of Supervision

One mother came to see me at my office, asking for direction. Her son had been referred to me many times for minor offenses, and I warned her that he needed rules and supervision—particularly from the time he came home from school until bedtime. She shrugged her shoulders. She had a job and couldn't see any way her hours could be changed. That summer I read in the paper that her son had been killed in a crazy game of Russian roulette with neighborhood friends.

Teenage years are information-hungry years, and teens deserve to have their questions answered with solid information that they can experiment with in nondamaging ways. This doesn't mean that teenagers should never be alone. It *does* mean that "alone" time should be on a continuum with "together" time in which teenagers and parents share information about times apart rather than lead separate lives. It also means that parents need to seek information, where appropriate, when their teenagers are under the supervision of other adults or older children. If that information seems to be vague, parents should be suspicious.

Lack of Experience

Teenagers are in the most vulnerable time of life, and they will make many mistakes through inexperience. David's encounter with explosives was a mistake. So was Connie's collision with the back of another car. She didn't have the experience to know how to handle a car on slick, icy roads. Her mistake cost us $200 and a substantial increase in insurance premiums; it cost the insurance company $1,700. Connie learned a lot from the mistake: that at age sixteen she did not know everything about driving, that her mistake was too great for her to personally pay for and would mean that the family would have to forego the new couch she had been hoping for, and that we, her parents, were legally responsible for the damage even though we hadn't committed the offense. From that point on she never questioned our driving or curfew rules.

Disobedience

Teens need to know the difference between a mistake and a sin. Deliberate disobedience is a sin.

We had an inexpensive electric car, which saved us a substantial amount on gas. Sherri took the children to school in it every day. It was incredibly easy to drive, requiring only a turn of the key and a foot on the accelerator—absolutely begging to be used. David and Steven, ages thirteen and nine, drove it from time to time around our big yard, though they had been told explicitly never to touch it. The moment of truth came, however, when they accidentally dented the fender going around the corner of the fence. Then they had to own up.

In the conference that followed, we asked them if they remembered the rule about the car. They remembered. We reminded them about Joseph Smith's practice of teaching correct principles and then letting people govern themselves. They remembered that, too. We told them that we realized they needed practice in governing themselves before moving out into the world, but that governing oneself took maturity. Unless they were capable of governing themselves, they couldn't have opportunities mature people had. We asked them who they thought should govern them: us, society, or themselves.

It was a bottom-line test. A lifetime of lip service to principle could be helpless in the face of intense immediate desires. David and Steven realized that their desire to drive that car had been greater than their desire to govern themselves according to a correct principle.

The discussion caused some tears and serious reflection. When we asked the boys what action should be taken, their answer was, "We *are* old enough to govern ourselves. Just wait and see. Leave the key in the ignition. No matter what, we will never touch it again until you give us permission. And you just tell us how much it is to fix that dent and we will somehow earn the money to pay for it."

It cost $400, and we knew they would never be able to pay for it, but we did assign some pretty heavy tasks, which they carried out faithfully. We paid the debt, but they made restitution. Since that time they have never touched that car without our express permission. We feel that we can trust them now, not only in this area but probably in some others as yet untested.

We knew that the future would bring many intense desires that could be controlled only from within. Our daughters are now on their own, and David is physically strong—there is no way to control them externally. But because we began early, with preventive discipline, we see with joy the strength of their own internal controls.

5

Teaching Correct Principles

One night I dreamed I was walking along a country road with David and Steven, ages fourteen and ten. As we came around a bend in the road, there before us was a huge black bear. When it caught sight of us, it reared up on two feet and moved toward us threateningly. For some reason, I knew that the bear did not have power to harm me but was bent on destroying my sons. Their only hope was me. I immediately put myself between them and the bear and told them to start running as fast as they could.

I woke up in a cold sweat, adrenalin flowing. To this day the dream remains as vivid as if it had really happened. Seeking to know what the bear represented, I instinctively felt that my sons were in danger because they did not have the firm understanding of the gospel they needed. They had not yet developed a love for the scriptures and an understanding of Church doctrines. My dream told me that this teaching was my responsibility.

My sons were born under the covenant. Our family read the standard works together in early morning devotionals, we attended church faithfully, and listened to the general conference messages twice a year. Yet it was clear to me that the boys needed something more.

I hadn't had the same feeling about our daughters. They had somehow caught the spirit of scripture study while still in Primary. Looking back, I can see many factors that accounted for this. Their mother worked in the Primary the entire time they were in it, and when the oldest daughter entered Young Women, Sherri accompanied her into that organization. She knew the manuals our girls were being taught from, taught them all the songs in the Primary songbook, and reinforced at home what they learned at church.

Before each of our daughters was baptized, we made sure she had read the Book of Mormon and was taught the significance of the sacrament. On the day of her baptism each girl received a new dress, a complete set of scriptures, and her own updated Book of Remembrance. It was a reverent and memorable occasion, and when each daughter was confirmed on the Sunday following her baptism, her spirit communicated that she was aware of the sacredness of the moment.

In seminary our daughters were attentive and serious and earned good grades. They loved their teachers and often discussed with us what they had learned.

We were gratified to see the influence the scriptures had on their lives. First Thessalonians 5:21-22 strengthened their resolve to avoid dating young men of questionable character. The concept of avoiding even the appearance of evil gave them courage to walk out of indecent movies and ask to be taken home. Second Timothy 1:7 helped them overcome their fears of recitals, important tests at school, and job applications.

When they received their patriarchal blessings, they kept copies of them with their scriptures as a reminder that these were their own personal revelations from the Lord.

Kathy, our oldest, bore her testimony to whoever would listen. A boy who rode her bus listened to her testimony every day, coming and going from school. In junior high they became good friends and before long he was taking the missionary lessons. As a result he was baptized, converted his adoptive parents, and served a successful mission. When Kathy invited her non-LDS friends to our home, she insisted they join us as we knelt around the table for prayers and then read the scriptures. At age ten she visited a Bible school with a friend and delivered a brisk

lecture on the nature of the Godhead. Before she graduated from high school many of her friends had joined the
Church.

Carolyn was much the same. Asked to give a speech in
English class when she was a junior in high school, she
outlined the plan of salvation on the blackboard and
explained it in detail. Her speech was to have taken seven
minutes, but the class and the teacher started asking questions and the discussion lasted the entire hour. Three years
later this same teacher approached my wife and asked
about Carolyn. When she was told Carolyn was at BYU, she
hugged my wife and said, "I just want you to let her know
that because of her speech that day, I began investigating
the Church. My husband and I have been members now
for two years, and we couldn't be more grateful. Please
thank her for introducing me to the gospel."

For our sons, however, family scripture reading was
something to be endured rather than enjoyed. Receiving a
new white shirt and suit for their baptism didn't excite
them. In fact, while our daughters' friends reinforced
them with oohs and aahs on their lovely day, the boys were
made to feel a bit sissy for having to dress up. Reading was
a delightful accomplishment for the girls, a chore for the
boys. Singing the hymns was "girls' stuff"—even in Primary.

In short, the approach that worked with our daughters
did not work with our sons. Study or discussion with Sherri
somehow seemed to prove to them that the gospel was for
girls. They obediently attended early morning devotionals
and did their share of the reading, but the lively discussions
passed over their heads. The boys attended church, but as
they moved into the Blazer group and into the priesthood,
they reported the disturbances made by the other guys,
saying that they felt unpopular if they even acted like they
were listening. It wasn't macho to know too many answers
in class. The positive aspects of church meant basketball,

hiking, and Scout camp to them. Even memorizing the Articles of Faith was a strain.

My dream about the bear crystallized in a powerful way a number of uneasy feelings. It became clear to me that if our sons were going to learn the gospel they would have to do so from me—and I would have to present it in such a way that they would feel personally benefited. Sherri and I had long discussions. We fasted and prayed. Then we made some decisions.

The first thing I did was ask to have David as my home-teaching partner. I felt that home-teaching was important, and I didn't want to take the chance that someone else would teach him it was mundane and unimportant. I wanted him to feel committed to his families and to develop the habit of making regular visits. I gave him the *Ensign's* message from the First Presidency and asked him to study it, be prepared to bear his testimony about it, and add anything he felt would reinforce the message. Following my lead, he has taken his calling seriously month after month for the three years we have been partners. He now makes all of the appointments, checks on his families often, bakes treats for special occasions, arranges holiday get-togethers, and has definitely grown in his ability to plan ahead and follow through.

In another effort to teach, I bought a video recorder and told the boys that I wanted to experiment with it. I directed each of them to listen to the lessons and talks given at church each Sunday and to select some message they felt would be of interest to the rest of the family. On Sunday afternoon they were to record these messages on videotape for their own sons and daughters to learn from twenty years hence.

I was amazed to see how much they learned—and their leaders and teachers would have been gratified. The boys didn't like their appearance on video at first so they spent extra effort grooming for the camera, following willingly their sisters' lead. And seeing themselves on tape taught them a great deal about annoying mannerisms, speech problems, grammar, and voice inflection. Most of all, their fluency in expressing gospel principles developed quickly, and their memory and retention of lessons and stories increased weekly.

Their ability to think on their feet and to organize a gospel subject from introduction to conclusion led them to voluntarily accept opportunites to give talks at church and seminary. Instead of the usual, "What shall I give it on?" and "What will I say?" it was, "Hey, listen, what do you think of this?" They expanded their use of our Church books, gathering ideas and supportive scriptures for the topics they chose instead of relying on a compilation of two-and-a-half minute sermons.

Another thing that unexpectedly increased their spiritual understanding was our insistence that they continue taking piano lessons. We had decided at the beginning of our married life that every one of our children would learn to play the piano. Our daughters accepted the discipline without question and learned the skill. Our boys resisted from the start, giving token obedience but begging us not to tell their friends they were taking lessons. Their progress was painfully slow. My wife endured power struggles on the piano bench day after day with each of them. As our daughters progressed one lesson a week, for years our sons progressed one note.

We refused to give up on them, vowing to stay with it until they ran away, and they finally began to progress. Just before our eldest son entered seminary as a freshman, his ability exploded. For the first time he began practicing voluntarily (though he still swore us to secrecy). Everything began to click, and his playing improved dramatically. Before long he was playing for seminary; then he was called to be organist for the priesthood meeting. That was frightening to him, so I played the piano while he played the organ, giving him confidence and pacing his tempo until he began to feel comfortable playing for others. His little brother followed his lead and is now polishing off hymns in preparation for the day when he too might be needed in priesthood meeting or seminary.

Serendipity is a marvelous thing. By playing the hymns over and over in preparation for congregational singing, the boys began singing along to their own accompaniment—and, to practice under pressure, asked us to sing while they played. These beautiful gospel messages were now reaching our sons. One day David reported that his seminary teacher had popped a surprise quiz. Quoting Elder Boyd K. Packer's encouragement to sing a hymn when a bad thought entered the mind, the teacher asked each of his students to take out a sheet of paper and write the words to any hymn. "I was one of the few able to do it," David proudly exclaimed. It hadn't occurred to him that he was memorizing words to the hymns.

Brother Robert Cochran, David's seminary teacher, reinforced the students' progress in ways that appealed to David. His relay races, teams, game shows, contests, scripture chases with huge candy bars for perfect scorers, and special privileges given for extra effort all hooked David into the memorization he hated. Week after week, he and his mother were up late, laboriously memorizing scriptures for a test the next day—something he found boring and difficult and irrelevant. But slowly, over the year, we saw a change in him. A speaker in church would tell a story to emphasize a point of doctrine, and David would attach a scripture to the story. When we listened to general conference, David linked scriptures he had memorized to doctrines the General Authorities expounded on. A television show would spark a quick scriptural retort dispelling the "good looks" that camouflaged a false doctrine.

We didn't want David's progress to diminish when school let out, so during the summer we launched into an accelerated study of the life of Jesus Christ, and we read together the biographies of each of the latter-day prophets. This, too, had unexpected results. Because teenagers haven't lived long enough to project how today's actions will affect tomorrow's, it is difficult for them to see beyond the here and now. They need careful steering away from those situations that could destroy them, but they resist being told what to do—not because they are incorrigible, ornery, rebellious, or inherently disobedient, but because they feel invincible, powerful, capable of handling any situation that comes along. They instinctively want freedom so much that they will fight against anything or anyone that controls them—even if that control is for their good. Studying the lives of great men gave our teens the opportunity to live great lives vicariously. Through this reading they were able to understand the details of preparation necessary for ultimate accomplishment.

When my sons read how Joseph Fielding Smith made bread before going to work all day at ZCMI, and how he used to make pies for his children, they could more readily identify with me; I had worked for my room and board at BYU by cooking for the rest of the guys in the apartment, studying while the bread rose and baked. They no longer felt so picked on if Sherri gave them kitchen assignments when all their buddies were out racing. When they tried their hand at several sports and spent most of their time benched, they took heart from the story of Heber J. Grant, who was rejected by the neighborhood baseball team until he solved the problem by intensive practice.

When a close nonmember friend asked David some doctrinal questions, he was stuck for an answer. Reading about Wilford Woodruff's converting and baptizing six hundred people after two days of preaching in Herefordshire, England, humbled him and taught him that if he was going to give an intelligent answer to even one question, he had better get busy.

The boys read about Joseph Fielding Smith hefting two-hundred-pound sacks for a living—and later providing a wonderful home for his family and moving on to pilot a jet in his fifties. This gave meaning to the teens' mundane, dusty work; it wouldn't always be that way if they could just focus on preparing now for tomorrow. The boys complained about blisters on their hands from working until they read about President Spencer W. Kimball's milking cows and working so hard that his hands were blistered and swollen; he had to hold them up in the air to keep them from throbbing.

Reading about how Christ and the prophets were rejected by the ignorant and the wicked can comfort teens faced with peers who reject them because of their values. In fact, it can create a bond and a sense of kinship with the great men and women who have succeeded in spite of harassment and rejection.

Of course, getting a teenager to read is not accomplished without moans, groans, and other resistance. They will present, with drama and pathos, lists of all the more exciting ways they could spend their time. For instance, during one summer my wife set a morning schedule for the family of early morning jogging, piano practice, a good breakfast, and then a reading session at the table. Since I was gone to work by 5:30 A.M., she had the superhuman task of enforcing the schedule by herself. Eventually a protest committee approached me.

"Dad, she makes us read for thirty to forty minutes." Another piped up, "Yeah, and we have to stop at every page and tell what we just read."

"I know, and you aren't any help," said one to another. "You keep asking all those questions."

"Well, it is interesting—kind of."

"Great!" I said with gusto. "Forty minutes ought to be a minimum."

The committee dispersed quickly, fearing I would add

another forty. (One thing I've learned from teaching seminary is that when teenagers resist you, it's best not to pay too much attention. If you are sure they are just expressing independence and that the thing you have asked them to do is right, they are likely to feel cheated and let down if you give in.)

Shortly after our interview the prevailing attitude began to change. When I would come home for lunch during this period, the boys would proudly boast of their early morning activities: "I jogged three miles today, Dad"; "We finished reading about John Taylor"; "Guess what, I finished Third Nephi." They had forgotten that their mom had had to pull them out of bed by the heels, singing heartily while pulling T-shirts over their heads and shoving tennis shoes on their feet. They didn't mention that she had had to place a German Shepherd at one door and triple-lock the other, hide the TV, and muzzle the telephone before bringing the latest biography to the kitchen table following breakfast.

Of course, such measures are necessary for only a week or so. Once your teens get into the routine and know you mean business, they will settle into it without comment; before long they will be reading more on their own. Then you'll find them quoting this story or that in their talks, bringing home good grades on their seminary tests, and reporting they were able to answer questions in church. Their prayers are more sincere. They feel good about themselves.

The hardest time to read scriptures together is after a crisis such as a move or a change of schedule that breaks the momentum. Getting started again is never easy, and somehow it's even harder when one of the parents is unable to be there, which is often the case. Demands at work and church, illness, divorce, death, and many other things may prevent parents from reading together. I remember one summer when I had to spend five weeks completing classes for my doctorate at a university a hundred miles away. Sherri's letter detailing her efforts to keep the family at their scripture reading during my absence is a treasure:

> Dearest Ronald,
>
> Oh, the trials of a single parent! You just don't know how much easier it is when you are here. I'll be so glad when you can take over again. I led the family in scripture reading last night. We each took our turn reading the first two chapters in Matthew. So if anyone wants to know if we still read even when you're gone I can say, "Yes—remember June 28 when David was half-dead in the bathroom soaking in the tub right after gym?" Connie sat on one beanbag right outside the door just out of vision, Steven sat next to her on another beanbag, and I sat on the floor between the bathroom and the hall. I read four verses and then let Steven finish the chapter.
>
> When Steven started on the second chapter, Connie got upset and asked him who gave him the right to do all the reading—it was time she had her turn, you know. After a brief tug-of-war between the two, Connie finally managed to free the Bible from Steven, and she commenced reading, finishing the second chapter for us all. She was glad we weren't going for the third because *Twilight Zone* was just starting and she had her exercises to do.
>
> I then turned my attention to the task of reviving David, who had passed out in the tub. . . .

By the time I returned, the family had established an early-morning routine similar to the one we had had while I was there. Sherri communicated to the children a sure sense of direction and proceeded despite circumstances and oppositions, demonstrating by her actions the importance of the scriptures.

You may wonder how such a scenario could possibly communicate a sense of reverence and love for the scriptures, but it did. The invaluable habit was being set. In fact, our teens report that they feel as uncomfortable skipping the daily scripture reading as they do going without brushing their teeth.

Once in a while the reading generates discussions that bring the Spirit of the Lord so undeniably into our midst that the hope of it happening again is enough to keep us going. And breakthroughs in knowledge occur unexpectedly for one or another. Though we've read the material more or less mechanically, when we seek an answer, a scripture or a phrase pops up before us in a way we never thought of before, strengthening us when our need is greatest.

There is a spirit of unity in gospel-living commitment that removes the necessity of preaching. Our teens can see for themselves the importance of living according to correct principles, and when a question arises, we have a common point of reference from which to decide.

There is a sense of security in knowing we have followed the admonition to study and teach one another the doctrines of the kingdom. We feel more worthy to approach the Lord in prayer and more aware of his presence. This increases our faith and helps us pray with confidence. No one likes to belong to an organization that constantly makes them feel they aren't doing all they should. Even though it is a struggle to keep our efforts continuous and we encounter mountains of resistance at times, the payoff comes when we are listening to conference or reading a message by the First Presidency or listening to a talk in sacrament meeting exhorting us to read the scriptures. A side glance at our teens reveals a clear, satisfied gaze that confirms the importance of our efforts. The respect they feel for their church leaders is transferred first to us—for we are teaching the same gospel as the leaders and speakers—and then to themselves.

Self-respect is one of the greatest sources of independence in teens. It is a far better motivator than any external pressure. It helps them to reach the point where "have to" becomes "want to." The strength we provide as parents is then no longer as important as the inner strength they have developed, a strength that will serve them the rest of their lives.

6

The Power of Prayer

One morning when Connie was in the second grade, Sherri and I heard her crying in the next room. When I asked what was the matter, she blurted out between sobs that she was never going to school again. She was finding it very difficult to read and had been placed in the bottom reading group at school. She told us that her teacher was cross and got mad at her when she mispronounced her words, that the other children laughed and made fun of her, and that she couldn't take it anymore.

Quietly, Sherri asked her if it was important to her to learn to read. Of course, she knew that it was, but she just couldn't get the hang of it and didn't think she ever would.

"Connie," Sherri said, "reading is one of the most important things you will ever learn to do. Why don't we pray about it?"

They knelt by the side of the bed, Sherri's arm close around her; together they poured out their hearts to the Lord.

"Father, Connie is having difficulty learning how to read," Sherri said. "Her teacher loses her patience and the other children don't understand. Just for today, wilt thou bless her teacher that she will have the patience necessary to help Connie, and help Connie understand how difficult it is for her teacher to teach thirty-seven students. Bless the students with understanding and thoughtfulness, and help Connie to understand that they have not yet matured in some ways—and to be friendly and understanding until they do. And please bless Connie with a clear and active intellect. Help her to listen carefully and to forget what others might think and concentrate on learning. We know this request is a righteous one—vital to future learning and growth—and we know that Connie is trying hard to be obedient to thy commandments. Wilt thou grant her this request this day. In the name of Jesus Christ, amen.

"Connie, now it's your turn to pray. Remember, the Lord loves you, and your success is important to him. With his help, nothing is impossible. He has helped you many times before. Remember those times and thank him for them and then pray with the faith that he will help you again."

Connie prayed with all the fervor of a shy little seven-year-old. The Lord heard our prayers that day. The teacher *was* patient, the children *were* understanding, and Connie was able to concentrate and learn.

The next morning, however, anxiety returned. Connie asked for a repeat of the morning prayer. She brought home her books, and we three worked diligently together. Day after day, week after week, found Sherri and Connie on their knees together as the school bus rumbled up the road. Night after night we worked hard, side by side on the couch reading together. Her fear of school gradually subsided, and before long she began moving up through the levels—not only in reading but in every discipline.

She continued to work hard and pray, and she eventually passed through junior high with every scholastic and artistic honor given.

Entering high school, she elected to study challenging subjects: physics, chemistry, computer science, math analysis. They were extremely difficult for her, and only hard work and prayer helped her through them. When it came time for her college entrance test at the end of her junior year, she experienced another miracle. She took the test at a very inconvenient time. Performing for Education Week, she had to finish one show, leave at 11:00 P.M., and drive three and a half hours to the testing site. After four hours of sleep she was to take the test, return home, and perform again. She called on the Lord for help. English and history were easy enough, but then she got to the math section. She had struggled all year in her math analysis class and she wondered now if she could remember the formulas for solving the problems in front of her. Again she asked the Lord for help. As she attempted to solve the first problem, she said, she could see in her mind the page number of her high-school math book with the very formula she needed to solve that problem. When she reached the second problem, her mental page turned again to the exact formula needed to solve that that one—and so on, until she completed the section. She felt sustained and loved and blessed.

During her senior year she repeated the math analysis class to ensure that the knowledge would be there when she needed it in college. She realized that the Lord had filled in the gaps when necessary but would expect her to do as much as she could on her own.

Our sons train for three hours daily in competition gymnastics. They have told us that often they have called upon the Lord to sustain them during difficult moments. Sometimes the skin on their hands has ripped in the middle of a difficult move, and a quick prayer for the ability to endure until the move was completed has brought immediate relief from the pain.

When Wilford Woodruff was president of the Church he counseled, "Live near to God; pray while young; learn to pray; learn to cultivate the Holy Spirit of God; link it to you and it will become a spirit of revelation to *you,* inasmuch as you nourish it." (Annette C. Hullinger, *The Illustrated Story of President Wilford Woodruff* [Provo, Utah: Eagle Systems International, 1982], p. 45.)

We have taught our teenagers that the Lord will speak directly to them through the Holy Ghost. By not providing every answer for them, we have tried to help them build the faith to call on the Lord for guidance.

When Carolyn wanted to know whether to go to college here or out of state, we encouraged her to pray about it. We told her that we knew she had the capacity to determine the Lord's will through fasting and praying and that we would stand behind her decision. When Kathy was considering marriage and asked us what she should do, we explained that she must seek her own answer carefully and prayerfully. We knew that even though she was aware of our feelings about the proposal, if difficulties ever arose she would find strength by remembering the Lord's assurance that she was doing the right thing.

If we can even once help our children experience an answer to prayer, that experience may be the foundation of their own testimony of prayer. They can't experience answers if they aren't asking for them. We can lead them in specific prayers for the blessings they need, avoiding meaningless words and trite, overused phrases. (See Matthew 6:7.) Prayer is truly "the soul's sincere desire, uttered or unexpressed"; learning to focus on sincere desires eventually prompts introspection and promotes a spirit of commitment.

Think of the strength and independence teenagers garner when they have been taught how to pray. The scriptures admonish us to "pray always, that you may come off conqueror." (D&C 10:5.) If teenagers are praying over schoolwork, dates, career choices, missions, sports events, service projects, and personal problems and temptations, they will conquer the destroyer.

We've watched our teenagers ace their seminary scripture-memorizing tests when they prayed the whole time they were taking the test. (Of course, they had done their share earlier: "Give them to me one more time, Mom.") We've watched them pray for each other during sports events, recitals, and talks.

When a teenager is drawn toward righteous activities through verbally petitioning the Lord daily for help, there just isn't room for unrighteous activities. The Spirit strives with those who allow their hearts to be full, "drawn out in prayer unto him continually." (Alma 34:27.) Such teenagers will receive wisdom to solve their problems, skill as they work at developing their potential, protection from harm, and comfort when hurt and disappointed. They will feel strength, purpose, and divine guidance, and will need few if any external controls. Parents can build this foundation by first leading the teens through an experience and encouraging them to pray for their own specific blessings. Once they discover the power of prayer for themselves, they won't forget it.

If you and your teenagers are not close enough to pray together, then pray for them, as Alma the Elder did for his son Alma and as Mosiah did for his four sons. Never lose hope that the Lord will help your teenagers discover that they can personally control their own destinies by learning to commune with Heavenly Father, seeking and then carrying out his will. After all, isn't that what we really want for our teenagers? We search for ways to help them bypass temptation, not only to ease our own sense of guilt when they transgress, but for their eternal joy. There is also great satisfaction in feeling that we have assisted the Father and the Savior to "bring to pass the immortality and eternal life of man." (Moses 1:39.) Only then can we experience companionship with a soul who was once our brother or sister in the premortal existence. That is parenthood at its apex.

7

Councils and Goals

President Harold B. Lee said, "Planning is the nearest activity there is to Godhood." We have certainly experienced the importance of planning in our own family. It has helped us become more productive, strong, and happy.

To plan together as a family you need to be together without distractions. When plans are made during dinner, for example, emotions, table accidents, or even the taste of the food may get in the way of understanding or committing to a particular goal. A family council can create the necessary focus; each new session provides a new beginning and an occasion to evaluate the past. Because councils are frequently held, goals, if accounted for and persisted toward, will eventually become habit, particularly when results provide an incentive.

To pattern the council after Church councils, you should take minutes or make some effort to record the goals. When goals are actually written down, they are easier to remember and are there as daily reminders. Regular councils provide definite time periods in which to reach goals. When a person has a definite goal to accomplish in a definite period of time, he is much more likely to achieve it. Teachers at school give due dates for tests, assignments, and term papers. Why not apply the same principle at home?

The Church has many different kinds of councils for different purposes, and the family can operate the same way. There should be councils between husband and wife, councils between both parents and one child, between one parent and one child, and with the whole family. Also, councils can be called to accomplish different purposes. Consider the following organization:

Annual Councils

In our family, we meet at the beginning of each year as an official Zirker Family Organization. We give assignments to each child to complete during the year. The purpose of these assignments is to serve the family in some way.

For example, when Kathy was still home I assigned her to compile our family history and update our scrapbooks, certificates, photos, news clippings, and other materials. Sixteen-year-old Carolyn was assigned to lead us all in physical fitness, and Connie, age twelve, was assigned to be music chairman and cultural refinement leader. David, at eleven, was assigned to be physical facilities chairman, supervising the yard work and fattening up our calf. His seven-year-old brother Steven was assigned to be education coordinator. He was to select good books to be read to him and ask someone to listen to him read. My wife was selected as nutritional chairman and learning skills coordinator in addition to her duties as home manager. I announced my plans to be financial chairman and head of the ways and means committee.

The results:

We have stacks of scrapbooks, with more accumulating. Carolyn charted us all on losing weight and doing physical fitness routines, introducing the gold, silver, and bronze award system. We presented twenty dollars along with gold medal status, ten with silver, and five with bronze. Our children earned part of their Christmas gift money this way.

Connie accompanied our singing weekly in family home evening, won several achievement awards with her violin and piano, won the leading role in the school musical, and organized the family "Singing Strings" quartet to enter Lehi-in-Concert and play in the Lehi Stake Orchestra.

David fattened up the calf and led in our own family butchering session. We filled our freezer with roasts and hamburger, cut, ground, and wrapped by us. We also painted fences, pruned trees, weeded, mowed, and planted under his direction.

Steven, who was poor at reading, advanced three levels in one year and was read to every night before he went to bed. He heard every scripture story in the standard works and the *Friend* month by month, cover to cover.

Sherri helped us eliminate all mix buying, taught the older children how to make everything from scratch, and worked hard to eliminate doctor bills through good eating. She assigned our daughters to alternate weeks baking bread and gave them complete charge over the Sunday meals. Each child was assigned chores to be done before leaving in the morning. All those over twelve were assigned to take care of washing, ironing, and buying their own clothes.

I managed finances, getting us completely out of debt. I paid for insurance, a wedding, a funeral, some home repair, college tuition for myself during the summer, and the hundred and one other necessities a family requires.

Semiannual Councils

Every fall, just before school starts, we meet to set up a schedule in harmony with each age and interest. It's tight, but with careful planning, everyone can meet his or her goals.

For instance, at our council for the school year 1980, Kathy had a job from eight to five, was enrolled in college classes at night, taught a children's choir, and was planning a wedding in the spring. She needed one of the cars to meet her goals.

Carolyn was a senior in high school, held a part-time job to which she needed transportation, was graduating in the spring, played the cello in the school orchestra, and belonged to a performing group.

Connie was in junior high, took piano and violin lessons, baby-sat frequently, and performed often with Bell Canto Strings and the Mesa Youth Symphony. She also entered regional violin competitions and played the lead in the class musical.

David played Pop Warner football, took bass and piano lessons, and played the bass in his school's orchestra. He also worked toward his Eagle Scout award, milked the cow night and morning, and sold extra milk and cream for his spending money.

Sherri was committee chairman for the National Convention of American Mothers coming to Arizona; she was also the stake Young Women president.

I was completing my doctoral requirements, serving as a member of the bishopric and as the stake admissions advisor for the Church Education System, working daily as a school psychologist, and managing property in Washington.

Each family member had household and outdoor chores. Each one had to clean his or her own room and one other room in the house, practice, and do outside daily chores before school. We got each child a calendar and had him fill them out for the year, including school requirements, concert dates, and holidays. Then we listed phone numbers of all the school teachers, music teachers, sports coaches, Scoutmasters, mutual leaders—everyone pertinent to each child. We placed the calendars on our kitchen wall with stick-on pens close by. All phone messages were written down on the appropriate date, along with the owner's assignments. New emergencies came up. David broke his arm. Grandpa died and we had to make several trips to Washington to settle his estate. Sherri's father died, leaving her mother needing extra help and concern. But we accomplished it all because we were organized and knew what was expected of everyone, and when.

Just before school is out we meet again to plan the summer. That particular summer of 1980 I had to attend Northern Arizona University for my doctoral residency for five weeks. Connie and David attended youth camp, July called for a trip to Washington to clean up our farm from the volcanic ash deposited, and we spent a week at BYU's Aspen Grove, where I was a guest lecturer. It may sound exhausting, but day by day it actually went quite smoothly.

Quarterly Councils

Preparing for the seasons makes them much more memorable—especially if everyone is in on the planning, preparation, and implementation. In October, we made our house into a haunted house for all the neighbors; at Thanksgiving we hosted forty-five relatives at our home for dinner; during the Christmas, Valentine's Day, and Easter seasons we prepared appropriate music and entertained at numerous functions together as a family. Looking forward to, planning, and anticipating holidays, we are less likely to feel life rushing by without tasting and savoring any of it.

Monthly Councils

Each Fast Sunday I have personal priesthood interviews with each of my children, taking note of how they feel and what they need, and then I follow through during the month (see chapter 13). Connie complained of having no place to keep her valuables so little brothers wouldn't get into them, so I took her shopping for a strongbox with a lock and key. David confided that he was the worst ball player in Little League; I set him up at the batter's cage and planned daily practice sessions with him. Steven cried that he never got to be alone with me; I planned occasions when he could.

Sherri is executive secretary. She checks over the month with each child and makes notes on what he or she needs: new shoes, a concert dress and our attendance at the concert, school projects due, recitals to prepare for. For years she had the children write their goals for the coming month in her journal, then checked on them the following month, writing new goals or redefining old ones. It was exciting to see one person's goal become the family's. When Kathy wanted to be able to swim a mile, we all wanted to swim one. When David began running four miles a day, Connie started joining him; now she is in the habit every day and her mother and Steven have joined in. Everybody became involved in David's goal to conduct a blood drive and learned that it takes hours and hours to perform a service we all take for granted.

Weekly Councils

We teach gospel principles weekly in family home evening and set goals to improve behavior. One valuable aid has been to derive behavioral objectives from conference talks, post these objectives for six months, and evaluate our progress at the next conference.

We prefer to spend family home evening totally alone rather than including other families. We didn't even invite Grandpa to join us, though he lived with us for five years. It is a private time spent in the spirit of the following counsel:

> When several families meet together regularly to hold family home evening, the purposes of the home evenings are defeated. These purposes are: to learn to talk to and listen to each other, to discuss frankly their own intimate problems in connection with living the gospel, and to strengthen love and unity in their own particular family. It is impossible to do these effectively

when several families meet together, for each family is different and its needs are different from those of any other family. The home evening should meet these unique and personal needs. (*Priesthood Bulletin*, March-April 1966, p. 2.)

President Kimball said of this time together, "The Lord has offered an old program in new dress, and it gives promise to return the world to sane living, to true family life, to family interdependence." (*Improvement Era*, June 1965, p. 513.)

Our most intimate and cherished memories are of time spent together, with the phone off the hook, enjoying a love that transcends the daily irritations of family life. Such moments provide the spiritual and emotional strength sufficient for any crisis.

Daily Councils

We hold our daily family council twice a day, and it is the most important one of all, for that is when we approach our Father in heaven together. President Brigham Young said, "Family prayers that request divine help in preparing children to go on missions, marry in the Temple, avoid evil, and display honest clean behavior have an influence for good on both the children and the parents in those family circles."

We have found it appropriate to kneel following a few moments of reading the scriptures together. One leads us all in prayer about general matters concerning the family and the world, and then we pause for several moments while each adds private comments he or she wishes to share with the Father. Even during those early years when our youngsters were toddlers, they would remain quiet, pudgy arms folded, though no one spoke.

We've learned to make a daily chart to spell out the day in detail and do our remembering for us. All of the children have had such a chart since they were old enough to read. Some don't need the chart anymore; activities have become second nature. Half the battle in any goal-setting program is remembering what you planned to do, carving it up into small daily proportions, and accomplishing a little each day.

Our youngest wakens at five o'clock, is dressed and on the piano bench till six, then comes to the table for scriptures, breakfast, and prayers. He cleans his room and one bathroom, brushes his teeth, and finishes any homework needing completion or heads outdoors for a game of ball— all before the school bus comes. He never goes to bed at night until he has set everything out: comb, hair dryer, socks, shoes, and coordinated clothes. He has watched his older brothers and sisters and set his own standards.

Selecting Goals

Priority goals are those that refine our ability to live the gospel of Jesus Christ. We have found that by listening to the conference talks every six months and listing each commandment emphasized, we have developed a list of those commandments most vital to us in this particular time period.

We try, by example, to teach our children that when the prophet says to "do it," we do it! There is no other alternative if we hope for the blessing. When he admonished us to clean up our environment, we did. We painted our fences. David and Steven are required to keep the lawn mowed and the place looking clean and neat. We've all done our share of weeding, pruning, raking, and cleaning. Our teens have seen us go regularly to the temple. Each child is expected to keep his or her Book of Remembrance up to date; volumes that have been kept over the years now fill our home. Each family member keeps a journal; these early entries of Steven's are pithy little memoirs he's already glad he recorded: "Wednesday, October 3, 1979. I went to Jimascixs. I was scerd but know that I cod not cri. Now I cept it and I felt glad"; or "Last nit I took a shawr and I dint haft to."

Goals should be varied to maintain balanced living. The personal and family preparedness program stressed by the Church suggests goals in career development, financial and resource management, education, physical health, home production and storage, and social, emotional, and spiritual strength.

Goals should be appropriate to the person. Some may be learning to read or play the piano, some to date, others to crawl. Also, each person has a different mission, different attributes to develop, and different weaknesses to overcome.

Meeting Goals

Goals need to be identified with the end in mind. For instance, Connie decided she wanted to be able to play a certain piano piece at the school talent show. Goals need to be written down with an approximate time limitation: Connie's talent show was six weeks away. An outline of what it will take to reach the goal must be made: Connie decided she would have to spend at least fifteen minutes a day learning and practicing the piece. If another person's help is needed, then this must be scheduled too: Connie asked for help at her weekly piano lesson and then scheduled the family to listen to her practice from time to time. However, goals should eventually lead to independence: Connie knew she would be able to play her piece well only if she could free herself from having to look at the music. She certainly didn't want a metronome there or her mother counting the beat. And finally, the most worthwhile goals include service: Connie did play the piece at the talent show, and also has since entertained with it often.

Who makes the goals? This depends on the child's age.

The fortunate child is one whose parents have set goals for him from the beginning, for many goals are best made before a child is born. The whole idea of parenthood is to lead the young ones to adult independence so that they in turn can guide their young ones.

The Lord's plan was to place a veil over our minds to see if we would obey the commandments and make something of ourselves even when Heavenly Father wasn't around. However, Satan was cast out of heaven, and no veil was placed on his mind. He still knows those noble and great ones who made commitments to serve the Lord on the earth, and he is determined to thwart those commitments. The Lord gives us a fighting chance by withholding Satan's power from the new ones, giving us eight years to teach them first. A child's brain is fully developed by age six; logic and reasoning are matured by age eight. If parents wish to be effective, they will set patterns during the first eight years in the areas in which they want their children to achieve: prayer, scripture reading, obedience, learning, family life, developing talents, work, keeping the commandments. The list goes on and on.

If patterns are not set before the age of eight, success is not impossible, but you will have the downward pull of Satan to fight. You will need even greater spiritual commitment and communication because your older children may find it more difficult to listen to you. After age eight they learn best through cause and effect, experiencing the consequences—and that can sometimes have drastic effects that are difficult to overcome.

When is the best time to make goals? When you have just been inspired, uplifted, and are feeling capable and committed. Goals will then lock you into positive action during the down times—and meeting them tends to inspire you to do so again.

Years ago, Sherri was challenged in a Relief Society meeting to do something uplifting in her community. With small children at home, she wondered how she could possibly accept that challenge. After asking the Lord to help her come up with ideas, she felt impressed to check with the local newspaper to see if they would be interested in a weekly column on rearing children. She loved to write and felt that a half-hour at the typewriter wouldn't detract from family life and might give ideas to some of the parents whose questions I heard daily. The editor reluctantly agreed to publish the column, saying that other citizens had tried such things before but usually gave up just as it was going well.

She began the column first under the title "Family Forum." Later, under different circumstances, she changed it to "Recipe for a Happy Family." It was fun for the first few months, but keeping it up week after week became something of a chore at times. We were committed, however, not wanting to be like those citizens the editor had spoken about.

The column has now been running fourteen years, and though it has never been easy, it has been extremely satisfying. One woman called recently to thank Sherri for an article on self-esteem and personal worth. Feeling alone and depressed after being released from a mental institution, she read that article and immediately had copies made for all of her friends in the institution she had just left. She said it had lifted her out of a blue day and gave her hope she hadn't felt in years. The mother of a child with Down's syndrome called to say she was ready to give up until she read our article telling about another valiant mother who persisted with a brain-damaged child and eventually found success. These experiences have given us the incentive to stay with it.

Why is it important to set goals? We are told that we were found qualified in the premortal existence to be God's governing ones on this earth. (See Abraham 3:22-23.) Read your patriarchal blessing; it will probably tell you of your mission—of commitments you made before you came here. You will be going back someday to account for the time you spent on the earth. What will you say you accomplished?

In June 1965, President David O. McKay, meeting with a small group from the Church Physical Facilities Department in his Hotel Utah apartment, said:

> Let me assure you, brethren, that someday you will have a personal priesthood interview with the Savior himself. If you are interested I will tell you the order in which he will ask you to account for your earthly responsibilities.
>
> First, he will request an accountability report about your relationship with your wife. Have you actively been engaged in making her happy and insuring that her needs have been met as an individual?
>
> Second, he will want an accountability report about each of your children individually. He will not attempt to have this for simply family stewardship, but will request information about your relationship to each and every child.
>
> Third, he will want to know what you personally have done with the talents you were given in the pre-existence.
>
> Fourth, he will want a summary of your activity in your church assignments. He will not be necessarily interested in what assignments you have had, for in his eyes, the home teacher and a mission president are probably equal, but he will request a summary of how you have been of service to your fellowmen in your church assignments.
>
> Fifth, he will have no interest in how you earned your living, but if you were honest in all your dealings.
>
> Sixth, he will ask for an accountability on what you have done to contribute in a positive manner to your community, state, country, and the world. (Fred A. Baker, Managing Director of the Department of Physical Facilities, handout by Anita Canfield during Education Week, June 1983.)

It is my testimony that what the Lord learns from us during that interview will determine his next action. Let us hope and pray and work toward hearing: "Well done, thou good and faithful servant . . . enter thou into the joy of thy lord." (Matthew 25:21.)

8

Excellence: No Excuses

When our son David was twelve years old, he broke his arm. Our hearts went out to him as we watched his pain, but three days of recuperating at home, plus the sympathy heaped on him at school, erased a good deal of the trauma. It wasn't long, however, before he came crashing back to reality. Reality was a broken arm in a cast that left only an inch of fingers showing, with term papers due, hunger that up to now only a deft right hand could alleviate, a cow to milk, and Scout camp to attend. Despair hit him hard, and he looked to his parents for the sympathy he was sure he deserved.

He first negotiated with me concerning the cow. Anyone could see that a one-handed milker was inefficient. Surely I would take over that chore for the next six weeks? Food would obviously have to be limited to milk shakes and pizza, something a lefty could manage; schoolwork would have to be given the benefit of a doubt (he would retire a month early); and he guessed Scout camp was impossible. He couldn't believe it when I listened sympathetically and declined to buy any part of the program, including milking the cow. "It will be inconvenient, son," I told him, "but it *is* possible. You can do it. You are *responsible* for doing it."

When he incredulously told his mother my verdict, Sherri recognized the old divide-and-conquer routine and said firmly, "If that's what your father said, that's what will happen, David. You *know* that." To me, she said, echoing his note of incredulity, "Ron, how *can* he?"

"Trust me, Sherri," I assured her. "I milked cows all my life—with broken arms, legs, ribs, you name it. He can do it. Let him know you depend on him. Don't buy extra milk. Show him you are grateful for what he does get and let him know that the family will make do with what he provides."

Nobody said a word at the table the first day he milked the cow, but the inch and a half in the glasses was eloquent. It took three days and a very uncomfortable cow before David realized I meant business. It really *was* going to be up to him! Within a week, a very proud son began bringing in buckets foaming to the brim. The satisfaction of seeing the family drink with gusto rewarded him daily.

Encouraged by that success—and the scarcity of pizzas and milk shakes—David became proficient once more at eating. He also began practicing writing and was able to complete his term papers legibly. By the time Scout camp came, David felt invincible. He not only went, but he single-handedly (literally) garnered six merit badges.

It was a tremendous experience to watch David learn he had greatness within himself. *I* knew he had it in him to succeed in spite of a handicap, but *he* didn't. Giving him the opportunity to find out, while staying close by to offer support, was hard on everybody but worth it. Since then, this knowledge about himself has encouraged him many times to persist when things got tough and he has been tempted to give up. It helps Sherri and me stick to our guns when we have thought through the decisions ahead of time, too.

The excuse "I can't" is crippling and cannot be accepted—especially in the face of so many examples of those who can. It is usually more honest to say, "I'm afraid to try," "I've only milked with two hands so I don't have the experience to know that I could milk with just one," or "I don't like to milk; I'm glad I have an excuse not to." What a boon it is to a young man to learn how to communicate to himself what he is feeling and why! That takes maturity, however, and parents should have more of it than their children. We've tried to teach our children the difference between being responsible for the things they can control (preparation for a competition, studying for a test) and not feeling guilty about results they can't control (the actual outcome of the competition). We've always tried to separate trying from succeeding. If you try a lot, you'll succeed a lot, but you'll also fail a lot. It's important to understand the process and not make excuses that will let you short-circuit it.

Another excuse that will hurt teenagers and keep them from progressing is, "I don't feel like it right now." I remember as a teenager going to bed once without feeding the cows and cleaning the barn. I was tired. I reasoned that it wouldn't matter just this once. About 10:30 P.M. my father shook me awake. "The calves are bawling, Ron. If they haven't been taken care of, then you must do it right away."

Several responses rushed to my lips, but in view of the incriminating evidence I didn't dare voice them. I had to get up and do my chores by flashlight. The calves were starving and twice as ornery as usual. It was twice as cold and very dark. All in all, the job took me twice as long. When I wearily finished the last task and trudged to my room at midnight, I had learned a lesson I never forgot.

Years later, I had the opportunity to teach a daughter the same lesson. It was twelve-year-old Carolyn's turn to do the dishes, and with her happy reassurance, Sherri and I left for an evening out. When we returned the dishes were still in the sink and Carolyn was sound asleep. It was 11:00 P.M. Sherri sighed and got out her apron. I stopped her, and we talked about it. Then Sherri went to bed and I woke up Carolyn.

Carolyn couldn't believe I would actually get her out of bed to do dishes in the middle of the night. She was stunned, resentful, and angry. Ignoring her groggy resistance and talking quietly and gently, I informed her the dishes *must* be done. What was more, because she had not kept her promise to do them, her duties would include every dish in the house.

Tears sprang to Carolyn's eyes as she plunged her hands into the dishwater. I pulled plates and tumblers from the cupboard until the drainboard was filled. Under her breath she murmured angry words that grew angrier with each dish. I stayed up the whole time with her—humming, reading the paper, sweeping up a little—and helping with a dish or two toward the end.

Late into the night when the kitchen was clean, I put my arm around her and sat down with her. Feeling genuine love and tenderness toward her, I thanked her for the beautiful job she had done. Then I said, "Carolyn, I know how angry I made you tonight. Well, your mother and I left you with your word that you would wash those dishes. They were *your* responsibility, and yet you took no thought of how your mother would feel when she had to face your dirty dishes before she could begin breakfast in the morning. She would have had not only her jobs in the morning, but yours, too. Carolyn, you are too precious and too special for me to allow you to behave in such a way. I want more for you than that. I want you to know the feeling of accomplishment when you have carried your load, done your share, and understood what others will feel about you when you don't. I don't want you to have to go through life believing that you aren't important—that what you do or don't do doesn't matter. There will be work to do in this life, Carolyn, that will not get done unless you do it. Never underestimate the importance of doing your duty—even when you don't feel like it."

Carolyn crumpled into my arms in tears, this time not hurt or angry tears. Years later, she told Sherri, "I never loved Dad more than I did that night!"

She was not an irresponsible person before that night, but she took a quantum leap in maturity after this concept of duty crystallized. She is the first to jump up if an item is missing from the table. She makes bread without being asked and cleans out cupboards on her own. Her loyalty to duty flowed over into other aspects of her life as she practiced second-mile service at school. She is now on a mission in Canada, and we have confidence she will serve with the same spirit.

There have been times when a child has let slip an improper word. When questioned about it, the excuse was, "I couldn't help it. It just slipped out," or, "I didn't mean to but when that hammer hit my finger. . . well, I hear my friends say it so much it just came out." Or worse, "You should be glad I'm not like my friends, Dad. I only say it when I get mad. They use those words all the time!"

What they were trying to tell me was that profanity is all right under certain circumstances and that a little is better than a lot. Needless to say, these are excuses we do not accept. President David O. McKay spoke clearly on the subject: "No parents can consistently teach faith in Christ who profane the name of Deity. . . . Blasphemous exclamations drive out all spirit of reverence." (*Gospel Ideals* [Salt Lake City: Improvement Era, 1953], p. 420.)

On occasion I have shared this experience with my family: My father and uncle owned a sawmill, and during the summer of my fifteenth year, I went to work for them. I had to get up early, sawing and hauling logs till late in the day. It was extremely hard work, tiring and dangerous. There was no way to avoid some of the scratches and bruises. Profane words flew like flies all day long. I learned enough words to fill a dictionary.

One morning, I arose very early and walked through the trees to begin work. Everything was quiet and still around me. I looked toward the east and watched the sun rise slowly, filtering through the branches of the beautiful pines and ferns, catching the dew on the underbrush. Birds were chirping happily, and other forest sounds blended with their chorus. I stopped to observe the beauty with a reverence and awe I had never felt before. Just then, a shouted expletive followed by several others rang through the forest as the other young men arrived to begin work. The contrast was so abrupt, so startling, so shattering, and so offensive that I made a vow on the spot that no one would ever hear me say a profane word.

Another excuse that never ceases to amaze me—and doesn't get far around our house—is, "But everyone else does it." This excuse covers attendance at improper movies ("I'll just close my eyes during the bad parts"), dances not up to standard ("I dance the same way I do at Church dances"), rock concerts ("*Most* of the songs are okay"), and drug parties ("Don't worry. I'm not going to smoke marijuana even if the rest of my friends do"). It covers immodest clothing, skipping school, cheating, and even shoplifting.

I hear these excuses more frequently from other children than my own, but I'll confess I am still shocked when I also hear excuses from parents: "It's just a phase they are going through." "That's a teenager for you." "If I don't let them do it, they'll do it behind my back. Better that it's done where I can be available if need be." Some parents say, "I don't like it, but there's no way to stop it. I just hope they'll grow out of it." Others will actually attend movies or concerts they don't let their teenagers go to, cautioning their sons and daughters to wait until they are "adult and responsible." How much easier it is to take advantage of those preteen years and never lose the control of a good example in the first place!

Another invaluable way parents can support teens is by not accepting excuses during the painful process of reaching a goal. Learning to pay the price for what you want in life is not always easy to do. It's not easy to teach. But it is one of the most important principles for reaching success.

When David reached about age thirteen, it became obvious that he needed something that was his own achievement. He knew it and we knew it. His older sisters had plaques and awards bulging their scrapbooks and covering the wall. Though he had given himself faithfully to the study of violin at age five, changing to the cello in fourth grade and to the bass in seventh, playing music didn't bring him the full sense of satisfaction or recognition he craved. He plodded along on the piano, joined Pop Warner football and Little League baseball, and felt the momentary thrill of suiting up and applying his wit and skill on the field. But he was one of hundreds of young boys and sat on the bench a good deal of the time. And even though he was part of a championship team one year, the season was soon over, leaving nine months with nothing to work for.

Even nine-year-old Steven had found his niche. We had enrolled him in gymnastics a couple of years before and discovered to our surprise that it was just what he needed to use up his excess energy and settle him sufficiently for quality schoolwork. His grades shot up, his confidence soared, and he entered competition training, spending three hours a day working out and bringing home several ribbons from every meet.

David and I talked it over. I asked him what he'd like to do. He said he didn't know but maybe it would be fun to try competition gymnastics, too. I warned him that gymnastics was a very demanding sport and that one of the biggest hurdles he would face would be to work as a beginner beside his accomplished younger brother. He agreed that everybody has to start somewhere, so we scheduled an interview with the coach.

He was crushed when the coach told him he needed to lose thirty-five pounds before he would even be considered for training. That just about stopped it right there—but I reminded him that all disciplines had requirements and that this was one he had personal control over. Still, the obstacle looked like Mount Everest. I said, "David, would you give me the opportunity to prove to you that you have what it takes to control your own destiny? If you will trust my judgment and do exactly what I tell you to do every day, I promise you that you will be on that competition team by spring. But you have to decide first of all if this is something you really want. If it is, I want to prove to you that you have what it takes to achieve it."

He didn't really believe me, but he said, "Yes, I really do want to get on that team. I really do!" So we set a goal that within six months his weight would be acceptable to the coach. Then we researched ways to get in shape. Locking the refrigerator looked like the first step. But a physical examination indicated that his metabolism needed to be changed and that running would be the most effective means to accomplish it. Together we visited a running coach, and he gave us important pointers on the type of running shoes to buy, the best way to avoid shinsplints, and strategies for David to gain proficiency steadily and safely. We shopped for shoes, shorts, and sweatsuits. We put his schedule on the calendar.

Then I asked the big question: "David, are you *sure* this is what you want to do?"

"You bet," he replied.

"There are going to be times when you are going to want to quit. If you do, you'll lose the opportunity to become a member of the team. Is it still your goal to try to get on the gymnastics team?"

"It's still my goal. It's something I've just got to do," he said.

"What do you want me to do if you are tempted to give up?"

"Dad, keep *all* of the wrong foods away from me and never, never give in, even if I act like I might want to quit."

"There are going to be treats everywhere you go, David. I won't always be around to stop you. You'll have to control what you do if you want to reach your goal. There will be days when you'd rather do anything but run—but running is something that you must do regularly or all your effort will be ineffective. Will you accept my efforts to keep you at it even when you don't feel like doing it?"

"Yes, Dad, I need your help."

I knew what was coming and he didn't. I knew he would be hard hit with muscle soreness. There would be rainy days, competing activities, a favorite television show, extra homework, and a hundred other excuses not to follow through on his plan. He had nothing to serve as a reference that consistent effort would pay off. I had to get his verbal commitment that he would accept my strength when his ebbed, because he was in for one of the most grueling experiences of his life, and it would take both of us to keep him running until he discovered that setting goals and accomplishing them was something he was capable of. I knew that if he didn't learn that now, he might go through life full of lame excuses, believing erroneously that he was incapable of success.

The plan was to start by running a half-mile the first week, move it up to one mile the next week, alternating with a half, and to gradually work up to between four and six miles a day, five days a week. Food would consist of items from the four basic groups—no desserts or goodies, and nothing after 5:00 P.M.

Scouts offered pizza feeds, sundae-building parties, and barbecues. David's school celebrated every holiday with gala, calorie-laden treats. His buddies devoured three hamburgers, two shakes, fries, and pie for school lunches. He would sit there with salad.

Running after school was an adventure at first. I tried to run with David but realized my physical condition called for a build-up at a slower pace. I couldn't restrict him on my account. I tried driving him a mile or two from home and letting him run back, but one day he came in sooner than usual without looking flushed, then admitted some good soul had felt sorry for him and offered him a ride. He needed steady companionship on the track. So I tried several things. I rode next to him on a bicycle, or put my car in low gear, turned up the radio, rolled down the windows, and slowly chugged my way beside him. I carried a water jug and vaporizer he could use to keep from getting dehydrated. His daily discipline became mine.

Excuses began flooding in after three weeks. The adventure was gone and he always felt winded and tired. Nothing seemed to be happening. There was complaining, pleading, resistance. I developed an acute case of deafness and kept a firm upper hand every single day. The hardest part came when he finally arrived at the four-mile run. That took time and stamina he was sure he didn't have. Just the mathematics intimidated him. But I held him to it, and his body finally began to respond. His waist went down five sizes. Six weeks short of his six-months goal he had lost thirty-five pounds, could run with ease and stamina, and looked like a million dollars.

Together we visited the coach. He said, "I'll put him in recreation gymnastics first for three months to see if he can work up to the moves he needs." David no longer needed prodding. He had passed a superhuman test already. Within one month he was ready for the competition team.

"How hard do you want to work, David?" the coach asked.

"I want to put in extra time so that I can catch up with the rest of the team in as short a time as possible," David answered. School was just about out. How would he feel about working six hours a day throughout the summer so he could try to be ready for meets during the coming year?

"I'll do whatever it takes."

David didn't understand what he was asking for. Six hours a day put terrific pressure on his hands. Sherri and I treated rips nightly. There were many days he was tempted to give up, but the memory of the previous year kept him going. Every morning he had to be at the gym by seven o'clock and would work there steadily till one. He still had his lawn-mowing and money-making projects to do, kept up a reading program, and worked toward his Eagle Scout, taking a week off for the big Jamboree with general authorities in Flagstaff. (He came home with eleven merit badges.)

When school started that fall he had mastered a lot of skills, and the coach decided he would take him with the team for his first practice meet in November. Any person with lesser commitment would have quit at that point. He was the lowest scorer on the team and had to suffer the humiliation of struggling with each move in full view of his teammates, who walked away with all of the honors. But he had learned what it felt like to be scored under pressure before judges and spectators. He stayed with it. I encouraged him, hoping he would at least be good enough to be able to compete at the state meet in April, but his performance in November left me worrying.

Then I used the video recorder—and real progress began taking place. I filmed his practice meets, and then together, his younger brother included, we watched each move in slow motion. We had the coach spot trouble points to look for: toe not straight, not enough angle on the spread of the legs, drop-kick too awkward, not enough time holding a handstand on the parallel bars. These tapes were about the only thing he watched throughout the preparation season. He and Steven were rapidly closing the gap between their gymnastic skills, and they became special companions, sharing hard and triumphant moments together. I went with David frequently to watch his three-hour workouts after school and headed the parent booster team that earned money to pay for travel and uniforms.

The meets began in earnest shortly after the turn of the year. The boys drove or flew to Idaho, Nevada, California, and all over Arizona attending meets almost every Saturday. I went with them to almost all of the meets and filmed their routines.

Week after week went by, and David's scores got higher and higher until pretty soon he started bringing home his fair share of the ribbons. By March, his score was high enough that he could be entered in the State Gymnastics Federation Competition Championship Meet. A dream had come true. Even though David figured he didn't have a chance his first year to win anything, he felt it a great honor just to be good enough to be in the meet.

On April 30, all of the teams met in Tucson and the meet began. The coach warned the team members in advance not to look at their scores until the meet was over because a low score might depress them and throw their next performance. David was so sure he didn't qualify for any awards that he changed into his jeans and team T-shirt before the awards ceremony.

Six places are awarded for each event, starting with the sixth first. When the first five names were read and his name wasn't one of them, David knew he had figured right—until they announced his name as the gold medal winner: first on the still rings, first place again for the floor exercise, silver medal for second place on the parallel bars, another gold medal for the pommel-horse, and again first place on the vault. For the final event, the high bar, they called him up for third place with a bronze medal.

We couldn't believe it. Seeing him stand there on the platform as they placed the medals around his neck made our hearts leap clear across the gym. When they announced him as the 1983 All-Around USFG Champion for highest scorer in his division and placed the fifth gold medal around his neck, we were all completely overwhelmed.

We knew that the medals meant much more than the fact that he had outscored his competitors. They symbolized his knowledge that success comes at a price and that he had what it took to pay the price. He had learned lessons about himself that would last forever. And he knew he hadn't done it alone.

As a parent, the experience confirmed for me that I could be influential in a way no other human being would ever take the time to be. Teenagers sometimes need the tough kind of faith from us that literally won't let them give up until after they've experienced success for themselves. Until they *know* that they can succeed, who will be their support system but parents?

9

Excellence: No Exceptions

The last chapter showed how parents can help teenagers develop a taste for excellence by not allowing an undercurrent of excuses to wash away their resolve. We as parents also feel responsible for teaching our children standards of excellence—not just music, but the best music; not just recreation, but the best recreation. Here again, we're grateful to have had those preteen years when the desires for experimentation could be channeled upward toward achievement and proficiency. We needed that time to allow our children to test *themselves* rather than to turn their energies outward in a test of the rules or downward in repeated tests of physical sensations.

We've felt a great need to be both firm and supportive as parents, for our no-exception standard has frequently confronted a "just-this-once" alternative. It has been a challenge to make saying yes to family standards more rewarding than saying yes to teenage friends.

In many families, teenagers' music is not defined as a problem as long as "how loud" can be negotiated. We accept and respect those families' choices. But in our family, we have chosen an absolute ban on most popular music, not only because we see negative elements in it but because we want the very best music for our children.

We came into our living room one day to find five-year-old Kathy and her friend gyrating enthusiastically to some rock music they had been able to find on the radio. Though we had never shown a liking for it, our daughter obviously didn't share our value.

We took a long look at the future. Kathy's delight was

not a one-time occurrence. It had appeared when she was a toddler. We fasted and prayed about it. Coincidentally, an article in the *Instructor* by Alexander Schreiner included a list of his hundred "best" pieces of music. The concept clicked: if we wanted to safeguard our children from the temptations that could come through rock music, we should teach them to appreciate the good. We took his list of the great classics and began collecting them. We had a fine stereo, but went a step further, installing an intercom system that piped sound into all the bedrooms. We played music for at least an hour every night, accompanying baths, back rubs, stories, and prayers.

We also bought tickets to community concerts and religiously took our children to all of them. Their reaction was one of boredom at first—and so, frankly, was ours. Our children would fall asleep during a long violin sonata, yawn and squirm during a cantata, whisper frequently, "Is it time to go home yet?" But we kept at it, dressing them in their best clothes, stopping afterward for an ice cream cone, doing what we could to make it a pleasant experience.

We kept at it: going to concerts, playing music at bedtime, starting the children on piano and violin. It took three years before we began to like it. We then began to notice our piano player. She would be wide awake, watching every movement of the concert pianist's fingers. And our violinist would crane her neck to catch all she could of the visiting artist.

Our daughters have now passed through the teen years, and though they whistled a popular tune now and then, rock music never became an issue in our home. They have never desired to watch the television midnight specials or asked to attend a rock concert. The pictures on their walls, by their own choice, depicted Christ instead of rock stars. They have never purchased any rock music. Gift records remained unused. Instead, their own talents flourished and the music of the stereo takes second place to their own.

Every note confirms to us that the Lord is willing to teach us how to lead our children in righteousness if we will ask.

Obviously, this long-range, intensive plan could not have worked if both Sherri and I had not been equally committed to it. Such experiences have helped us to develop a great faith and trust in each other. Together we are worth more than we are apart. For instance, years ago we were called to be a fellowshipping couple in a new branch of the Church—and we had no idea where to begin. There were no instructions, no manual, but we were told that one was coming and to do our best until it came. We did not feel that our calling was in suspension until then. We fasted and prayed to know how to carry out our stewardship. Ideas flowed thick and fast, and we worked diligently to put them to good use. Imagine our feelings, when the instructions finally arrived, to find that they were identical to the ideas we had received through inspiration!

We've used this model when our children haven't been quite sure where to begin. Principles aren't always clear at first. A book of instructions isn't always available. Where it is, it should be followed closely, but where it isn't, we are entitled to inspiration that can be received only through fasting and prayer. We are thrilled to find our children asking us to fast with them for enlightenment about their own decisions. This kind of independent relationship with Heavenly Father is a great strength in their decisions to reach for excellence with no exceptions.

When sixteen-year-old Connie was asked to join a group of friends at a party, they asked her to bring her own car because they knew she would have to be home before the party was over. As it turned out, Connie was home less than an hour after she left. The party was a dance that did not meet her standards.

It had not been a hard choice for her; her real test had come years before. Just a few weeks after her fourteenth birthday she had been invited to a friend's for an evening party—her first. She had looked forward for months to group associations and went in high spirits. She returned home early in the evening, very downcast, and went to her room. The next day, after sacrament meeting, when she felt calmer, she told us the story:

The day before the party, she had traveled with a busload of other teenagers from neighboring schools and communities to an honors regional music festival. On board, the conversation turned to current movies—who had seen what? She hadn't seen most of them. Why? "They're R-rated, and I don't go to R-rated movies."

They were incredulous, teasing, "I'll bet you will when the time is right." She vigorously shook her head. Then, just one night later, her friends at the party put on a videocassette of an R-rated movie. She told us, "I sat there for about five minutes. It felt like an eternity. What should I do? 'I'll *never* go to an R-rated movie' ran around and around inside my head like a broken record. I finally decided I either had standards or I didn't, and to just sit there was making a statement—to my friends, to myself, and to the Lord." She asked to be taken home, and a very disgusted friend complied.

"It was hard to embarrass my friends and cause them inconvenience," she said, "but I was so grateful I could partake of the sacrament with clean hands and a pure heart and have the Spirit confirm that I had done the right thing."

We knew how hard it must have been—it is hard for us, too, sometimes, to turn off an entertaining show that becomes crude or profane. But if choosing the show was a mistake, to continue watching substandard material would be a transgression. The excuse "How did I know it was going to be so bad?" is only valid up until the first bad moment.

I don't feel I can take a chance on shutting the Spirit out of my life for even a day. It's hard enough in this telestial world to get it and keep it. I depend on it too much to deliberately choose something that alienates it. I'm not saying that people who make different decisions are unrighteous, but I do know what the consequences would be for me.

We have tried to define appropriateness in the media by what we want it to do for us. Are we asking to be entertained, educated, informed, moved to action, proselyted? All these expectations are worthy of our time if the material edifies. We are told in Doctrines & Covenants 50:23, "That which doth not edify is not of God." Even if the media is not particularly offensive, it can cause bickering, waste time, substitute for parental guidance, or create a fantasy approach to life. Some who watch game shows daily feel covetous and discontented. Some who watch soap operas are disappointed and resentful that their own marriages lack such "romance."

Some parents use questionable material as the basis for a discussion about right and wrong. We have occasionally done the same, but we've usually found that the answer is very obvious—so obvious that the lengthy drama made out of it obscures the question. Some parents reason, "If I don't let them watch what they want here, they'll go someplace else and watch it anyway." If our children do this, we feel that the transgression is then upon their own heads— but to allow such material in our home is to condone it. Even if our children reject our values, at least we have made it clear what those values are.

What if your teens defy you? It has been our experience that teens are extremely sensible and just. They can understand reasoning and have a sense of fair play. I also believe teenagers have strong moral spirits that recognize truth and steadfastness. Their immaturity may cause balking and irritability at times, but they respect those who expect excellence from them.

I remember when Kathy invited a group of friends to a

slumber party to celebrate her thirteenth birthday. "Oh, good, 'Saturday Night Live' will be on," they said. "I'm sorry," Kathy had to tell them, "but we'll have to watch something else." No one showed up. That was tough on Kathy. We tried to be close, to share her disappointment and express our pride. But underneath, I wondered how she was really taking it. The next weekend, she invited another group of friends over to a baking party; the goodies would be delivered room to room at a nearby home for the elderly. Everyone showed up and had a wonderful time. Both incidents anchored her conviction that the "popular" media didn't have to be part of her life.

This book includes a lot of negative examples because crises make values very clear—but in day-to-day living, we rarely mention what we are against. We are *for* a lot of good, exciting, growth-promoting things. In an atmosphere of progress, excuses die from lack of nourishment.

With so many foster children in our home, our children have seen firsthand the results of "just this once." They visited Ronnie in the detention home and saw the holes he had mashed in the walls of his cell from the frustration of being locked up—a bright and handsome fourteen-year-old with too much free time and no supervision.

We feel deeply that our children have the right to hear us witness for the truth. We don't have the right to change that truth so that they will like us better, even if they rebel against us and deny that truth. Where else but from us will they learn of their greatness, their foreordained missions, their ability to call upon the Lord for strength to rise above handicaps or weaknesses, their birthright of excellence without excuses or exceptions?

Our commitment to the truth doesn't mean we don't love and accept our children. It does mean we can never give our permission for them to do something contrary to what the Lord expects of them. It means that we can accept no exceptions to excellence.

10

Dating Decisions

Dating can be a problem for teens, and decisions about dating seem to bring otherwise harmonious parents and children to the point of conflict. In our family, we've handled dating exactly as we've handled all situations for which counsel from the Church exists. The principle is certainly clear enough: group activities after age fourteen, double- or triple-dating after sixteen, and single-dating after mission age. Long before our children were old enough to face the situation themselves, Sherri and I reviewed the principle to be sure we both understood it the same way, and we committed ourselves to help our children obey it until they had a testimony of it themselves. Our firmness and commitment meant we probably weren't assailed as persistently as we would have been if we had wavered, and it is that firmness that Kathy and Carolyn have specifically thanked us for over and over. "Whew!" they've said. "We really could have gotten into some bad situations if we'd gone out before we did. By the time we turned sixteen we sure had a lot better sense."

Kathy, now married in the temple, cradles her daughters and son and exclaims, "Oh, Mom and Dad, I can see now how much you hoped and prayed for me to do the right thing. It would hurt so much to see little Charity or John Paul get into trouble. I want to keep them safe and pure and good."

Carolyn, preparing for her call to the Canada Winnipeg Mission, emerged from the temple in tears, grateful for her worthiness. Both the older girls' testimonies have deeply influenced their younger sister and brothers.

Though they have faced many trials, they have kept both the spirit and the letter of the law, at times risking friendships and popularity.

It was especially hard for Connie at age thirteen. Many a night she came home from school in tears. "Everybody else" was going to a boy-girl party. It was also hard for her at age fifteen; many of her friends were "going steady," and no one had even asked her to! What if no one *ever* would? "I know what I'd say," she wailed, "but I don't even have the satisfaction of saying it!"

Night after night, Sherri or I sat on the edge of the bed, rubbing her back and letting her talk. We assured her that the reason no one asked her out was because they knew her principles. If she'd be patient, the finest young men in town would be standing in line. This time was hers to learn about dress and grooming, and about real conversations on interesting topics, and to develop her talents so that when the season arrived she would be worthy of the very best!

She followed our advice—running four miles a day, practicing her violin two hours a day and the piano for another hour. She got top grades. And sure enough, since the day she turned sixteen, young men we are proud to associate with have asked to share her company. In spite of the rule about doubling or tripling (we offered to be the second couple if necessary) Connie has missed only one prom. Her date couldn't find another couple to double with, and his parents had the same rule.

We have other rules, tried and tested with Kathy and Carolyn: no steady dating till after missions, a midnight curfew on weekends, places of entertainment that meet family standards. Chastity has not even been a question, and the barriers are formidable to those with unsavory intentions. Many of their friends, both boys and girls, have the same rules, and group gatherings, rather than formal dates, are popular.

When David announced his plans for a coming-out party—dinner and dancing at the Hyatt Regency, with transportation in Mom and Dad's brand-new Oldsmobile— we didn't try to let him down gently. "Whoa," we said. "With whose money?" Then we pointed out what it would mean to a girl he asked out if she knew that he was saving his money for mission and college funds, and if she knew that dating time was at a premium because he was aiming for academic and athletic excellence.

"Don't you think she'll be just a little flattered, David, if you let it be known that you're kind of choosy, and that the girl you marry is going to have the best in life—a man who has served an honorable, productive mission and whose plans for the future include excellent preparation for a worthwhile career?"

Sherri's mother-son talks about why she'd been attracted to me—a quiet farm boy but a hard-working returned missionary bent on a degree—were also impressive, since he has a hard time imagining a woman with either perfections or beauty his mother doesn't have.

Understanding his fear that a sharp girl might not want to go out with him unless he could take her to an exotic, expensive place, we encouraged him to think about the kind of girl he wanted to marry. Would he really be interested in the girl who pouted every time she couldn't have everything she wanted? If he carried out his long-term plans, it might mean years of sacrifice until his education could be obtained. Did he want to be united with his wife in their goals or to be struggling with immature selfishness? Besides, wouldn't he love knowing that a girl liked him for himself—his charming and thoughtful personality, his clean and virtuous habits, his sense of humor, and his creative ability to make an inexpensive date more fun than an elaborate one—rather than for expensive dates?

We warned all of our teens, particularly our daughters— in hearing distance of our sons—to beware of any guy that came on with a fancy car and expensive dates. Was his father footing the bill? Would his father always be footing the bill? What was he like without *any* support?

Any girl who would persuade a young man to abandon his goals just so she can have immediate pleasure will reap disappointment, for she is announcing that she will settle for second best. And a young man is obviously not much of a man if he is willing to abandon righteous plans and personal commitments.

When our eldest daughter met Greg and they made the decision to be married in the Mesa Temple, they had a detailed plan for completing both of their college degrees. They worked out a schedule at BYU that would allow them to help each other in case a baby arrived, arranged for medical insurance that would cover pregnancy, bought a used trailer with cash, and arranged a twice-weekly paper route to pay for the trailer space and utilities. Greg's job as night custodian at the Provo Temple brought in enough for groceries. They submitted their completed four-generation family group sheets and pedigree charts, refinished furniture, collected enough items for their living accommodations, bought a two-years' supply of basic food items for four people, and embarked on their life together totally independent.

Charity arrived ten and a half months later and accompanied them to classes. John Paul was born shortly after Greg graduated. They sold the trailer and set the money aside for law school, worked a summer in preparation for more expenses, and replenished their two-years' supply of food.

They found an apartment house close to the University of Utah that they could manage in exchange for rent, and they earned money to cover the utilities by collecting all the rents on time.

When they wanted a date, Greg took his spray can and metal number forms to a residential section of town and hired himself out to paint addresses on curbs. With the proceeds they hired a baby-sitter and went out for dinner and a movie.

Their second daughter, Rachel, came shortly before Greg's graduation from law school. Kathy, who had kept up her education through correspondence courses, needed only ten credit hours to finish her degree. Debt free except for a student loan, Greg was prepared to move into the community to begin his law career. Neither partner had compromised priorities, nor did they forfeit cherished goals and ambitions. Kathy had fulfilled her role as a helpmeet, and he had been the provider: not the Church, not the family, and not welfare.

President Kimball advised, years ago: "One can have all the blessings if he is in control and takes the experiences in proper turn; first some limited social get-acquainted contacts, then his mission, this his courting, then his temple marriage and his schooling and his family, then his life's work. In any other sequence he could run into difficulty." (*Ensign,* February 1975, p. 4.)

Hard? Yes. Worth it? Oh, yes. And it started with those also-hard and also-worth-it dating decisions.

While Sherri was stake Young Women president, one of her projects was a "Creative Date Book" that proved quite popular with teenagers in our area and set their own creative juices flowing. Here are their dating ideas—all of them tested by the teenagers themselves.

Creative Dates for Social Development

—In the mail, I received a homemade coupon that said, "This coupon entitles you to a luxurious superdate. If you accept this offer, please sign and return this coupon at once to ———" I returned it, and he picked me up and took me to his house. His mother was dressed like a cook and his father like a first-class waiter. After we ate, his father chauffeured us to a special play. It was really fun because I got to know his parents too!

—We had fun eating a picnic lunch at the airport terminal, watching the planes take off and land.

—We took seven other couples and went fishing in my uncle's pond.

—We had dinner where everyone did everything backward.

—To get into the party you had to bring an inexpensive or homemade gift and a potluck dish. After dinner, everyone blew out the candles and ate as the presents were opened.

—We went Christmas caroling on Halloween with five other couples. We finished with a "Halloween Silly Supper." We had to order from the following menu only three things at a time (not knowing what they were):

Ghoulish Goulash . . . (Soup)
Bloody Veins Pilaf . . . (Spaghetti)
Deviled Delight . . . (Deviled eggs or cake)
Spooks Spectacular . . . (Cream Salad)
Skeleton Bones . . . (Fork)
Owl Eyes . . . (Cookies)
Screaming Cats . . . (Spoon)
Witches Brew . . . (Punch)
Flying Bats . . . (Knife)
Leering Masks . . . (Chocolate Cream Pie)

—Get some fluorescent golf balls and play in the dark.

—Have a pancake or waffle dinner at your home. Suggested toppings are:

Strawberries and whipped cream
Maple syrup with pecans
Creamed gravy with chipped beef
Orange sauce with powdered sugar
(Boil 2 cups orange juice; add ½ cup sugar and bring to a boil again. Soften 3 tablespoons cornstarch in 2 tablespoons water; stir into boiling mixture till thickened,

using a wire whisk. Add a glob of butter and serve hot over pancakes or waffles. Sprinkle with powdered sugar.)

—We had a pizza party and asked each guest to bring part of the topping. Roll out thawed frozen bread dough, or prepare regular pizza dough. Go creative with toppings and decorations.

—I took my date to her house and her parents helped us build a cookie monster out of homemade cookie dough.

—Make out a crazy questionnaire of things to do. Have your dates fill them out, and then do those things they circle on the questionnaire. (The party that did this played volleyball and horseshoes, and then sang.)

—After a dance, several couples came over and baked huge chocolate-chip cookies (as big as a pie pan). Then they spread ice cream on top of each, piled on the whipped cream, and put a cherry on top, and several couples took bites from every side.

—Each brought his or her own cake, different shapes, any kind. Frosting and decorations were provided. The best-decorated cake got a prize; then cakes were auctioned off at the ward dinner with money going for youth activities. (One sold for $26!)

—We had fun eating a spaghetti dinner with every utensil except a fork.

—We bought ice-cream cones and then counted how many licks it took to finish them.

—We reversed roles and the girls drove and paid.

—Checking with parents beforehand, the young men knocked on the door at 5:00 A.M. The parents told their daughter to throw on some old clothes quickly and answer the door. When she did, a blanket was thrown over her head and she was carried out to the car and taken to the desert for a fun early-morning breakfast.

—Our daughter invited a friend and the family for dinner. She sat us down at a picnic table covered with a red-checkered oilcloth. First she brought salad and dumped it in the center. Next came hot spaghetti, which she arranged down each side of the salad and then covered with sauce and Parmesan cheese. She handed us each a fork, a napkin, and a loaf of piping hot garlic bread and set us to eating. It broke the ice and changed an awkward meeting of a special friend into laughter and fun humor!

Creative Dates for Intellectual and Cultural Development

—I hated classical music—at least, I did until my date took me to hear an organ recital. He said he hated it too before we went, but afterward we decided we both like it!

—We went to an art museum and pretended we were critics. People thought we were pretty funny.

—During the summer, most libraries show several top-rate movies free at their theater or at a grade school. Get the schedule by calling the local Parks and Recreation office.

—There are probably many places in your community that offer the use of their craft facilities for a small fee. You can learn ceramics, painting, drawing, pottery, stained glass, fibers, needlepoint, photography, woodworking, drama, and jewelry.

—Try out for your local drama production. There isn't anything more fun than developing a common bond through sharing such a continuing experience.

—Most museums are inexpensive or free. Make it a point to visit every one in your area. Have a treat after each visit.

—He took me to his house and gave me some coveralls, and we worked on his motorcycle. After we got it running, he took me for a ride.

—Most high schools have an orchestra or band and prepare at least three or four concerts a year. Most are free. Also, many communities have their own city orchestras or bands and present three or four concerts a year for modest admission charges.

—Plan ahead a special route on bikes. Eat the first course of dinner at one house, second at the next, ending with dessert and a good video at the last house. (Or reverse it, starting with dessert for fun.)

—Dress up like cowboys and cowgirls. Visit a ghost town and make movies. Finish later with a "showing," complete with popcorn and tickets.

—Choose a special event—birthday or departure—and prepare a scrapbook for that person: poems, essays, collages, pictures, and so on.

—Make a batch of cookies and invite those needing to pass the biology or history test over to study.

—Go to the library. Finish back at the house with submarine sandwiches or chili.

—Get acquainted with various occupations; visit such places as a citrus, dairy, or fruit farm; a glass, steel, or shoe factory; a cannery or a clothing plant; a grocery or banking business.

Creative Dates for Developing Physically

—We had games marathon style. Each couple was a team. We played table tennis, horseshoes, and croquet.

—Fly a kite and finish with a picnic lunch.

—We roller-skated all over town with three other couples, then skated to the ice-cream parlor. Another group roller-skated all over the high-school sidewalks.

—We made patterns in the grass with the mower.

—My date and I went with my parents to the mountains. They sent us on a hike and had dinner ready for us when we got back. It was fun, and I got to know my own parents better.

—My date and I went with four other couples to a

nearby hill on bicycles to watch the sunset. As the sun was going down, we talked about the things we were most thankful for. It was special!

—You may have to pay the Forest Service a small fee to get your own Christmas tree, but it's an incredible experience. Just wear warm clothing and waterproof shoes and let others know where you are in case of bad weather or other problems.

—The best date I have been on was a picnic in a cornfield. We ate, and then put on music and danced fifties dances. Afterward we played games we used to play when we were kids (Red Rover; Red-light, Green-light; and so on).

—The members of our priests quorum brought dates to the bishop's barn. We had a dinner and a square dance. It was a blast.

—We like to play football with our dates at the local junior high.

—We picked up our dates on a horse and took them riding around the rim.

—We played tennis about an hour and a half before sundown. The tennis courts were next to the track, so when it became too dark to see, we ran the track for a while. Then we sat on the grass and talked about our lives and our goals.

—We visited a cave.

—My date suggested we spend the evening seeing what we could do on less than ninety-nine cents. We first bought ten pieces of gum. We then bought a thirty-nine-cent package of birdseed and fed some birds in a park. Finally we bought some marshmallows and roasted them at his house.

—I've had the most fun with a great big group tubing, walking, and riding in the mountains looking at nature. Things like that are a lot more fun and uplifting than elaborate, expensive dates.

—Take a sightseeing tour of the city on bikes.

—Go to the park and play on all of the equipment. Finish with a hike to an ice-cream parlor.

—Wash cars. Don't wear white T-shirts.

—Take your little brothers and sisters to the zoo.

—Have a Frisbee chase in the park.

—Go to an athletic contest at halftime. You'll get in free!

—Have breakfast and a game of tennis before school.

—Go swimming.

—Play cops and robbers on horseback.

—Climb trees; play pool; have a water balloon fight.

—One is "It" in this game of water polo. "It" closes his eyes, counts to five, and then shouts "Marco." Everyone is then obligated to yell "Polo" while "It" tries to get them. Warnings to keep "It" from hitting the side of the pool are important!

—A large water-ball is thrown to members of team, who try to keep members of opposite team from getting it.

Creative Dates for Spiritual Development

—Read the scriptures on Sunday night. Add popcorn or punch and cookies and take turns reading.

—My three friends and I decided to ask three inactive girls for a date. Two of them are active now!

—We rented a BYU film for seven dollars and invited three couples to watch it with us. After the movie we talked for about three hours about the movie and our goals. Many great movies and filmstrips plus projectors (if a trained person is there to help) can be checked out from the meetinghouse library and shown to a group.

—Go to an older person's home. Work together in the garden, mow the lawn, and clean house.

—We had a surprise dinner for a boy in our ward who is going on a mission. He was the only one who didn't have a date. After the dinner, he told us why he was glad to be going on a mission. It was really uplifting and made me want to marry a returned missionary.

—We went to our ward genealogy room and looked up names and stories. At first I was embarrassed and didn't want to go, but it was really fun to read about some of those pioneer people.

—We walked around the temple grounds, then went to the visitor's center and saw the exhibits and movies. We listened to the guides and then shared our thoughts with each other.

—We went to a Church dance. Afterward we went to my house, fixed a sandwich, and went outside and talked about the beauty of the earth and how God has blessed us. We had a great discussion.

—Attend church or firesides together.

—Practice your seminary scripture chases.

—Play Scrabble, using Church names and places.

—Visit the sick, afflicted, homebound, or hospitalized.

Encourage your teenagers to try some of these dates or, better yet, to come up with some equally creative date ideas that will help them get to know their dates better while becoming better people. Dating, like most of life's activities, can be a powerful way to grow and to have fun at the same time.

11

Effective Interviews

Some time ago I discovered a principle of Church government that seemed made to order for parents who feared losing contact with their children. I discovered this principle—known as the personal priesthood interview—when I uneasily realized that even with my very best efforts and Sherri's unceasing work to keep the family running smoothly it still lurched along, barely chalking up a day without some contention here, some unfinished chores there, some rebelliousness elsewhere.

When these unpleasantnesses erupted, I found myself getting involved with the children (at that time ages thirteen to three) quite swiftly and directly. I understood my motivation: I wanted to be the power in my child's life—a force for good—even if it involved sharpness at times. It is true that my reproving really did bring us closer together when it was followed by "an increase of love" (D&C 121:43), but I was uneasy about this cycle of rebuke and affection. Wasn't there some way to keep things consistently positive?

Consistently positive. It suddenly came to me that family home evening, a real power in our family, was like sacrament meeting in exactly that way. We held it consistently every week, and its regularity gave us repeated chances to focus our lives on positive spiritual matters and set commitments for the coming week. And if home evening worked in that way for the family as a whole, why wouldn't a regular, consistent session with each child work too? Wouldn't it help take the element of crisis and contention out of the everyday contacts among individuals in our home? That was when the model of the personal priesthood interview occurred to me. I couldn't wait to try it out with my family.

But when? Holding interviews on Monday night before or after home evening meant uncomfortable time limits, even though it had the advantage of being a night when I never had any other commitments. Sundays I was busy early and late with Church assignments, except for Fast Sunday. Since we fasted from evening to evening and our testimony meeting was always held right after Sunday School, that left a long, hungry stretch of four or five hours.

So, resisting the urge to sleep out the long wait, one Fast Sunday I announced my desire to meet with each of my children that day. They naturally wondered, "What have I done wrong now?" Beaming, I assured them it would be a good time for them just to talk, to tell me their problems, ask for help, or otherwise use the time as they saw fit. Dubiously, they each came in that day with very little to say.

"Well, dear, how are things?"

"Fine."

"Good! [long pause] Any problems?"

"Can't think of any."

"Can I help you with anything?"

"Oh—I don't know. Everything is just fine."

That was when I learned my first lesson. Because I had set up a new and somewhat formal way of relating to my children, they were a little nervous and uncomfortable with the change, and so was I, even though some warmth seeped through the awkwardness. I kept thinking something was missing. What did my priesthood leader and I do in our personal priesthood interviews? I could remember feeling a little awkward the first few times there, too, a little reticent to set goals, to say what I felt. But we had prayer together. All right. Prayer! Next month, so would we— opening and closing.

"Prayer?" they said. "Just you and me?"

So the younger ones prayed that those who didn't come this time would come next time. The older ones stammered through a sentence or two, not quite knowing what to say. Come to think of it, neither did I.

But the Spirit was there. The children were a little less self-conscious. I felt good about just the consistency of following through by holding the interviews two months in a row. The children opened up a little more this time, but hesitantly. I responded by biting back all recriminations, accusations, lectures, advice, counsel. We focused only on what *they* wanted to discuss.

The next month, I had proof that they had begun to believe I was serious, that they really could say what they wanted, and that I really was available for their concerns. And I had the shock of my life. What I heard were unsparing criticisms of me as a father. Floods of them. Everything they had ever wanted to say came blurting out. They cried. I cried. I listened. I bit my lip and listened some more. I checked my feelings and listened again. Then I hugged each one, we prayed, and I called in the next one.

The family surrounding the table was quieter that evening. Eyes were soft, a little embarrassed, a little apologetic. I smiled. I didn't say a word. Their goodnight hugs were especially tender that night. I hugged them back. After all the things they said, they needed assurance that I still loved them—and I think they were trying to let me know that they loved me.

Their tenderness increased throughout the month, and a surge of excitement grew in me as Fast Sunday approached. What was the next one going to be like?

I should have been able to guess what would happen. Having released their feelings toward me, they now began to release them about the rest of the family. If their comments came out sounding selfish, they knew it was allowed. We asked the Lord (less self-consciously now) to help us discover our problems and find ways of overcoming them. A big problem, the teenage girls decided, was Mother—cross, unappreciative Mother. Someone else always got more attention; the younger ones had all the restrictions and none of the privileges. Again, I listened. I hugged. We closed with prayer. Around the table that evening were fearful faces, wondering if I would betray a confidence and talk about what they had said against each other. I smiled. I kissed each of them warmly that night.

Then Sherri went to June Conference—the historic last such conference in 1975—and came home bubbling about an achievement program titled "Behold Thy Handmaiden." She was anxious to implement the program in the lives of our Laurels in the stake, but she could also see the possibilities for our own teenage daughters, who were not yet Laurels. We discussed it and decided that after our daughters met with me, they would then meet with her to set specific goals: short-term goals for the next month and long-term goals for the coming year (see chapter 7). This meant extra organization, since she wouldn't have time to get dinner ready while we were having our interviews—but it was worth it to both of us.

She divided a notebook into sections, one for each member of the family. Then she wrote down the areas discussed at conference: spiritual awareness, homemaking arts, recreation and the world of nature, service and compassion, cultural arts and education, and personal and social refinement. In her interviews she asked each daughter to write down one thing she would like to achieve during the month in each area. The next month, they would evaluate the goals together, make new ones or renew old ones, and discuss other things done during the month that also fit any of the areas of focus.

The first obstacle was the vagueness of the goals. For spiritual awareness, one would say: Read the scriptures. One daughter was a good reader, and the Old Testament would be her seminary course of study the coming year. Predictably, that month she had read only a few pages of Genesis and was pretty discouraged. But the discussion pinpointed another problem: she had chosen a goal that she thought Sherri wanted her to choose. When she realized that she was really free to pick what *she* wanted to do, she came up with goals that were a lot more realistic—goals she was much more motivated to work on.

We all got caught up in helping the children achieve their goals. One wanted to sew a dress for her homemaking goal. Her younger sister hadn't set that goal herself, but she got involved and ended up making one for herself. Another daughter wanted to swim a mile without stopping. The whole family made it to the pool so often that three of the children mastered it instead of one.

It became so much fun that it kept spreading. Our boys were younger, but they participated in their own version. It made living together richer; our lives became filled with doing and growing. The children began to feel better about themselves, and they sensed our growing admiration and love for them. Bickering had been replaced with cooperation.

We are still having those monthly interviews, and I've learned for myself those conditions that have made them the single most effective thing we've done to draw our children close to us, and why they have been so effective.

A recent television documentary revealed that teenage suicides are epidemic. One of the reasons given was that teenagers don't have anyone they can talk to, anyone they can feel close to, who will be there when needed, who knows their past, loves them, and cares about them—yet whom they can go to if they are in trouble, whom they can trust to advise them, with their best interests in mind.

As a psychologist, I have met many teenagers who have expressed this same need and many parents who would like to help but don't know how. A clue from psychologists as to how they do it might be of value: One advantage they have is a set time and place.

I have found that teens or children don't open up to me until I've seen them several times. Also, it takes a lot of courage for them to risk a relationship by divulging some of their inner feelings, fears, trangressions, worries, and problems.

If there was a chance that what they divulged got around, they would never take that risk again. Also, if they thought it would spoil a relationship, they wouldn't feel safe talking anymore.

By following a few principles, I found I could create a climate where my children would feel safe in my presence to be themselves and communicate freely. These principles follow:

The Interview

1. Establish a set time and place and safeguard the privacy. (We use our bedroom, which has a lock on the door, and set the time for the first Sunday of each month.)

2. It is vital that no one else be allowed in the room but the two of you.

3. Get comfortable, but find a way for some contact: eye-to-eye, or a shoe touching theirs, your hand on their shoulder, a small child cuddled in your lap.

Touch is very important. It should communicate your love and the feeling that "our time together is very special to me!"

4. Ask questions that will give them an opportunity to express their honest feelings: "Is there anything on your mind that I should know about?" "Are you satisfied with your life at home?" "How do you feel about school, church, dating?" "Is there anything you need?"

5. Don't be discouraged if they respond only in a general way at first.

6. Remember to maintain your role as a counselor. Be an active listener. This isn't the time to be a director, teacher, judge, playmate, preacher, or diagnostician.

7. Watch for the nonverbal feedback: tone and pitch of voice, eye contact, and so on.

8. Your first session may be awkward and nonproductive. Don't give up.

9. When you sense they have said all they are going to, end the interview with prayer. (That is something you can do in your own home. No legislation against it!)

10. Follow up throughout the month. Find several ways each day to say, "You are special to me!" (A nudge, a wink, a note, a warm arm around the shoulder, looking straight into their eyes warmly, answering their questions, helping them with their problems.)

11. Don't betray confidences, ever! (A friendly talk around the dinner table about name-calling and how it hurts, with a wink in the direction of the offended, however, can let her know that her complaint was legitimate and that she has an advocate in her behalf.)

12. It's better if a child can get such attention from both Mom and Dad. (Even if they are divorced. Even a widow was able to draw her husband into the interviews she had with her children: "Your dad would have suggested that . . .")

In Luke 2:52, we read: "Jesus increased in wisdom and stature, and in favour with God and man." This scripture might be used as a guide for organizing personal interviews or counseling sessions with our children. We might ask about their progress in "wisdom," which includes how they are getting along in school, what plans they have for future careers, and how well they understand gospel principles; "stature," which may involve their feelings of self-worth, their physical and emotional health, even their personal appearance; "favor with God," including personal worthiness, spiritual growth, obedience to the commandments, scripture study, love for the gospel, personal prayers, and testimony development; and "favor with man," which may involve social development, relationships with members of the family, friends, employers, teachers.

The most important ingredient, however, is to communicate your sincere devotion to each child. Pray to know the heart of this brother or sister entrusted to you by the Lord. Pray for personal vision of his or her greatness and foreordained mission. Elder A. Theodore Tuttle has promised, "When we as parents have a genuine *desire* to teach the gospel to our children, the Lord will give us entrance into their hearts. Then may we know that as we enter there we stand on holy ground." (*Ensign,* May 1984, p. 25.)

My greatest moments with my children have been during our interviews. Now when we meet, we have prayer only at the end. Having it at the beginning seemed to focus our minds on problems rather than on feelings. I always make sure I am in some kind of physical contact with them. Many times they will lay their head in my lap or on my shoulder. That contact keeps the tone constant, warm, and tender. Their feelings flow; sometimes the tears do also, but through it, the touch remains steady and warm and tender. We are able to look each other in the eye when we are through, and then we kneel together. The specific blessings of the priesthood that each child needs are poured upon his or her head, and our fasting is dedicated to his or her special needs along with the family goal we have previously selected.

There is no doubt when the interview is over of the special love we share, and it is sweet—sweet enough to help preserve us from temptation throughout the month. I find myself wanting to give my life for them. They sense this and return my love for them by steadfastly living the principles of the gospel. Our family unity grows stronger every month; each part of the whole is in better working order. Sherri and I have found that our own communications are becoming more honest and accepting, too. As husband and wife, we've never been closer.

We look forward to Fast Sunday. There is a relevance to the fast that we never felt before. I see a glow of spirituality on my children's faces and my own spirit soars. I believe that I am experiencing fatherhood in a more complete way. Our children come to me throughout the month, trusting that I truly have their best interests in mind.

There is a simplicity in parenthood that has gradually become clearer in the twenty-five years I've spent with my children: They have always been willing to respond to me in direct proportion to the amount of love and attention I was willing to give them. And that love has motivated me to be worthy for their sakes far above what I might aspire to for myself. If I pray that they will not have to suffer the consequences of breaking the law, I must make sure I never break it. If I expect them to feel the accomplishment that comes from rising early with a clear set of objectives for the day, they need to see me doing it—and enjoying it. If I wish never to punish them for swearing, speaking disrespectfully to their mother, lying, or cheating, they must never hear me doing these things. If I am concerned about preventing vandalism, late-night cruising and boozing, or blatant disrespect for authority, I need to make home a place of peace, affection, and attention—one where they would rather be.

These one-on-one monthly talks have been my greatest tool for keeping communication open. The children's freedom to speak their minds, to ask any question, to pour out their hearts, knowing that the interaction will be totally confidential and that I will take great pains to clear up a problem or help answer a need, has built a bond of loyalty between us that I was not able to build any other way. They know there aren't any games between us.

Over the years this ability to relate to each other one-on-one has helped various of our children bring low grades to high, develop talents where there didn't seem to be any, overcome tendencies of laziness or sloppiness, prepare well for a successful future, and avoid harmful situations—and it has built the kind of love that makes it possible for me to imagine heaven.

Index

Dream, 40, 45
Driving, 18
Drugs, 26, 29, 31, 41
Duty, 77-79

Earning necessities, 19
Earning privileges, 14
Electric car, story of, 43-44
Enthusiasm toward gospel, 45-47
Environment, 22, 33, 69
Example, 69-70, 114
Excellence, 14, 92
Excuses, 14, 22, 76-77, 79-80
Expectations, 7, 15, 34
Experience, lack of, 42
Explosives, 15-16
Eye contact, 12, 111

Failure, parents' sense of, 21
Family goals, 64-65
Family home evening, 67-68
Family prayer, 68
Fast Sunday, 66, 107, 114
Fellowshipping couple, call as, 90
Finances, self-sufficiency in, 16
Forgiveness, 37
Foster children, 2, 3, 93
Freedom, 34
Frustrations, 4

Goal-setting, 15, 62, 64-65, 69-73,
    109-10
Governing of self, 43
Grant, Heber J., 51
Grounding, 19
Gymnastics: prayer helping in,
    59; Stephen's involvement in,
    81; David's work to enter,
    81-85; videotaping, 85;
    competing in, 85-86; David's
    winning, championship, 86

Habits, teaching, 12, 14, 41, 48
Handicaps, 76
Heredity, 22

Holiday, preparation for, 66
Home-teaching partner, son as,
    48
Honesty, 31-32, 77-78
Hymns, 50

Independence, 13, 16, 18-19, 60
Inexperience, 42
Influences on character, 22
Inspiration, 90
Insurance agent's son, story of,
    40
Interview. See Personal Priesthood
    Interviews

Jesus Christ, 7, 8, 51-52, 71
Jogging, 52, 82-84, 95
Journals, 69-70
Judgment, 38-39

Kimball, Spencer W., 52, 68, 98

Learning, transferring, 12
Lee, Harold B., 62
Lessons, learning, 1, 17, 32
Lessons, piano, 49
Letters, 3, 54
Lord. See Jesus Christ
Love: parental, 24, 30-33, 78-79,
    94, 113; unconditional, 26-27;
    familial, 37-39, 67-68

Marijuana. See Drugs
Marriage, 17, 36, 60, 96-98
McKay, David O., 7, 73, 79
Media, appropriateness in, 92-93
Mediocrity, 22
Messages, false, 31
Milking cows, 52, 75-76
Misbehavior, 10, 114
Missionary work, 46-47, 79, 94
Mistakes, 42
Money, 16-17
Monthly councils, 66-67
Movies, R-rated, 91
Music, 88-89

Necessities, earning, 19
Negativeness, 26
Newspaper column, 72

Obedience, 8. *See also*
    Disobedience
Organist, David called as
    priesthood, 49-50

Packer, Boyd K., 50
Parents, 7-8, 15, 31
Patriarchal blessing, 46, 72-73
Permission, 93
Personal Priesthood Interviews,
    24, 66, 107-9, 111-14
Perspective, 22, 32
Piano lessons, 49-50
Plan of salvation, 71
Planning, 13, 15, 62
Practice: piano, 49, 52, 69-70;
    gymnastics, 81, 84-86
Prayer, 9, 11, 57-61
Prevention of misbehavior, 10,
    114
Price, change requires, 28
Priesthood, 16, 38, 47, 49-50
Priesthood blessings, 16, 38
Primary, 45
Privileges, earning, 14-15
Privileges, parental, 32
Problems of child-rearing in
    scriptures, 1
Profanity, 19, 79
Professionals, consulting, 25
Prophets, 51-52

Quarterly councils, 66

Reading, 51-52, 57-58
"Recipe for a Happy Family," 72
Rejection, 28-29
Relationship, parent-teen, 24-25
Remedial steps, 11
Repentance, 27, 29-30, 32-33,
    35-38

Responsibility: of parents in
    scriptures, 1; independence
    brings, 19; not learned in
    childhood, 21; taking, for
    decisions, 30; of parents to
    teach gospel, 45; for chores,
    77-78
Restaurant, story of children
    walking out of, 31-32
Restitution, 31-32, 43-44
Rewards, 13, 34
Role of parents, 8, 15
Routine, 12, 53
Running. *See* Jogging
Russian roulette, story of, 41-42

Safety, 41
"Saturday Night Live," 93
Sawmill, experience at, 79-80
Schedule, 52-53, 68-69
Scripture study, 45, 47, 50, 53-54
Scriptures, 1, 4-5, 45, 50
Seasons, preparation for, 66
Security, 55
Self-centeredness, 11-12, 24-25
Self-control, 10, 19, 33, 43-44
Self-evaluation, 33
Self-image, 15
Self-respect, 55-56
Self-sufficiency, 17-18
Self-worth, loss of, 22
Semi-annual councils, 64-66
Seminary, 28, 46, 50
Service, 14-16, 70
Sewing, 17
Shooting accident, story of, 40-41
Skills, developing, 13-14, 17, 19,
    28
Smith, Joseph, Jr., 8, 43
Smith, Joseph Fielding, 51-52
Sons, teaching gospel to, 47-49
Speaking ability, increase of, 49
Spirit, divine, 38
Stages of development: self-
    centered, 11-12, 24-25; skill-